Easy
Knitted
Socks

Easy
Knitted
Socks

FUN AND FASHIONABLE DESIGNS
FOR THE NOVICE KNITTER

Jeanette Trotman

St. Martin's Griffin
New York

A QUARTO BOOK

EASY KNITTED SOCKS.

For information address
St. Martin's Press, 175 Fifth Avenue,
New York, N.Y. 10010.

www.stmartins.com

Library of Congress Cataloging-in-
Publication Data is available upon request

ISBN-10: 0-312-36199-8
ISBN-13: 978-0-312-36199-0

First U.S. Edition: May 2007

Conceived, designed, and produced by
Quarto Publishing plc
The Old Brewery
6 Blundell Street
London N7 9BH

QUA: EKS

EDITOR: Michelle Pickering
DESIGNER: Elizabeth Healey
PHOTOGRAPHERS: Andrew Atkinson,
    Sam Sloane
ILLUSTRATOR: Stephen Dew
PATTERN CHECKER: Eva Yates
ASSISTANT ART DIRECTOR: Penny Cobb

ART DIRECTOR: Moira Clinch
PUBLISHER: Paul Carslake

Color separation by Modern Age Repro
House Ltd, Singapore
Printed by SNP Leefung Holding Ltd, China

10 9 8 7 6 5 4 3 2 1

contents

Quick & easy projects

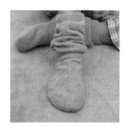

Introduction

The recent resurgence in the popularity of knitting has seen lots of demand for patterns for bags, hats, and scarves as knitters try to find the next small project to keep their fingers busy. Socks are often regarded as too difficult to tackle, but the fact that they are small, portable items that can be as practical or as decorative as you wish means that they are ideal projects to knit. This book aims to dispel the myth that sock knitting is difficult by taking you through the projects step-by-step.

For new sock knitters, projects like the lacy top-seam socks (project 14) and stripy Fair Isle socks (project 19) combine the use of lace and slip-stitch techniques with short-row shaping to produce simple socks knitted on two straight needles. As your confidence grows, projects like the basic tubular socks (project 8) and mock-cable socks (project 18) will become less daunting, and you will quickly discover that working on double-pointed or circular needles to produce your first socks in the round, complete with turned heels, is both achievable and fun.

Along the way, projects like the butterfly and bumble boots (project 4) and felted Sunday boots (project 5) will make clothing the feet of you, your family, and friends lots of fun. Once you have completed your first project, you will wonder why you haven't tried sock knitting before—you'll be hooked!

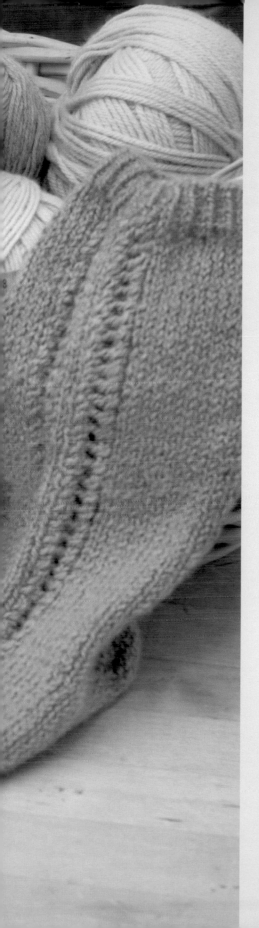

Tools, materials & techniques

THIS CHAPTER PROVIDES GUIDELINES ON THE TOOLS AND MATERIALS YOU WILL NEED TO KNIT SOCKS, FROM CIRCULAR NEEDLES TO SOCK YARNS. ALL THE BASIC KNITTING TECHNIQUES ARE ALSO EXPLAINED STEP-BY-STEP, TOGETHER WITH AN OVERVIEW OF HOW TO CONSTRUCT A SOCK. IF YOU ARE COMPLETELY NEW TO KNITTING, PRACTICE THE TECHNIQUES IN THIS CHAPTER BEFORE STARTING ANY OF THE PROJECTS. IF YOU ARE MORE EXPERIENCED, USE THIS CHAPTER FOR REFERENCE WHENEVER YOU NEED TO.

Tools

All you need to get started is a pair of needles and, as long as they are the right size for the project you are making, you can start knitting. However, there are many other items of equipment that you may find useful.

DOUBLE-POINTED NEEDLES

Needles

Needles are available in a variety of materials; the cheapest are aluminum and plastic. They can also be made from bamboo, steel, ebony, or even bone. Different materials will give you a different knitting experience, and personal preference will dictate which you choose to knit with. If your hands tend to sweat when you knit or you suffer from arthritis, you may find natural materials such as bamboo or wood better to work with. It is important that the needles are not bent and do not snag the yarn while knitting. The thickness or size of a needle should also be appropriate for the yarn you are using. A needle gauge is a handy and inexpensive tool to double-check the sizes of unmarked or old needles. There are three types of needle: straight, circular, and double-pointed.

Straight needles

Unless specified otherwise, all of the socks in this book are knitted on straight needles rather than in the round, so they are perfect for beginners. Straight needles come in pairs and vary from 10 to 18 in. (25 to 45 cm) in length. Although socks are small, remember that you will probably want to use the needles to knit larger items in the future.

Circular needles

These consist of two short needle ends joined by a flexible plastic or nylon cord. They come in different sizes and the length of cord varies. They are used for working in the round so that you can knit seamless socks. High-quality metal needles like Addi Turbos allow the stitches to slide easily from the needle tip to the nylon cord, and are recommended when using the magic loop technique.

Double-pointed needles

These come in sets of four or five and have points at each end, allowing you to knit from either end of the needle and work in the round. They make it easy to change direction when turning the heel on a sock. Make sure that the double-pointed needles you use are short enough to make knitting in the round comfortable, but not so short that the stitches drop easily off the ends. A 6-in. (15-cm) long set of needles is perfect for a pair of socks.

Cable needles

These short double-pointed needles are used to hold stitches at the back or front of the work while knitting cables or tie stitches (project 18).

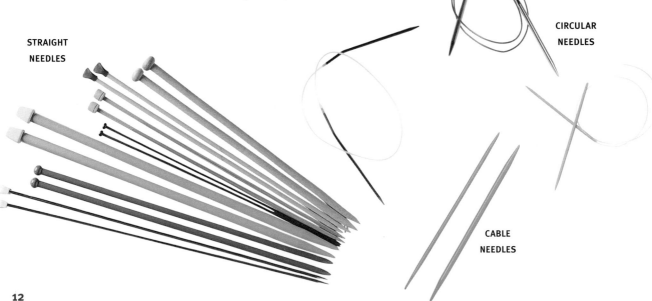

STRAIGHT NEEDLES

CIRCULAR NEEDLES

CABLE NEEDLES

COIL NEEDLE HOLDERS

ROW COUNTERS

POINT PROTECTORS

SCISSORS

TAPE MEASURE

Coil needle holders

Wrap a coil needle holder around sets of double-pointed needles to keep them together when not in use.

Tape measure

This is an essential piece of equipment for checking gauge and making sure that your work is the correct size.

Row counter

Place this on the end of a needle and turn the dial after each row to keep count of the number of rows worked.

Glass-headed pins

Glass-headed dressmaking pins are used to hold pieces of knitted fabric at the correct size when blocking and steaming.

Stitch markers

These colored plastic or metal rings can be placed onto a needle or into a stitch to mark a particular stitch or row. You could use scraps of contrasting colored yarn tied into a slipknot instead. Locking stitch markers fasten like little padlocks.

Scissors

These are essential for trimming the ends of yarn, particularly at the back of work, although it is better to break woolen yarns because the feathered ends from breaking are easier to hide when weaving in.

Sewing needles

Blunt-ended yarn needles come with different-size eyes to accommodate various thicknesses of yarn. They are essential for weaving in loose ends of yarn and sewing seams. Sharp sewing needles are useful for threading beads onto yarn.

Point protectors

Place these on the ends of needles when not in use to stop stitches from dropping off or to protect the tips of bamboo needles, which can chip or split.

GLASS-HEADED PINS

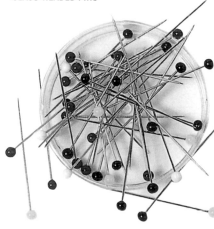

TIP: KEEPING A RECORD

Keep a small notebook handy to record yarns used, dye lots, personal gauge, felting notes, and so on.

STITCH MARKERS

SEWING NEEDLES

Yarn and other materials

The main material used to make the projects in this book is yarn. Although the specific yarns used are listed on pages 126–127, you may wish to knit a project using a different yarn. Understanding the qualities of the types of yarn available will help you choose one that is suitable.

SILK/COTTON BLEND

Yarn

Yarn is made by spinning fibers of natural and/or synthetic material together. The combination of fibers used produces yarns of different softness and strength, which affects the look and feel of the finished item as well as what the yarn is like to knit with. Yarn fibers can be split into two categories: natural and synthetic. Some yarns are a blend of natural and synthetic fibers.

Choice of fiber

Natural fibers are obtained from either animal or plant origin. Wool is popular because of its ability to keep out the cold and wet. Some wool yarns have been given a shrink-resist treatment, making them machine washable, while untreated wool shrinks or "felts" when machine washed, producing a fabric that is durable and can be cut without unraveling. Alpaca, angora, and cashmere are also popular natural fibers; they are beautifully soft but comparatively expensive. Natural fibers of plant origin include cotton, linen, hemp, and ramie/jute. These do not have the same natural elasticity as wool but are ideal for warmer temperatures because they are cool to wear. Synthetic fibers include rayon, acrylic, polyester, lycra, and nylon. Synthetic yarns are often machine washable and tend to be cheaper than yarns made from natural fibers because they cost less to manufacture. Some yarns have a synthetic element added to strengthen the natural fibers, making them more durable and helping them to retain their shape when knitted.

PLAIN AND SELF-PATTERNING SOCK YARNS FOR FAIR ISLE AND GRADED EFFECTS

COTTON

NATURAL-FIBER AND LUXURY BLEND YARNS

ALPACA/SILK BLEND

**KID MOHAIR/
SILK BLEND**

**VISCOSE/
POLYESTER BLEND**

Sock yarns

It is possible to buy special sock yarns. These are generally a sport-weight wool with a synthetic fiber added to produce durable socks with a snug fit. However, you do not have to use sock yarns to knit socks. Socks that are not made from special sock yarns and do not have a synthetic content will not be as hardwearing, but they are perfect for casual wear. When considering which yarn to use, think about when the sock will be worn and select the best yarn for that purpose. Whether you want light-weight socks for everyday wear, soft cashmere socks for snuggling on the sofa, or durable thick socks for hill walking, the yarn you choose should be right for the project you are knitting. Reinforcement yarns are available made from a blend of superwash wool with a 25 percent synthetic element. These can be worked along with the main yarn in areas of the sock that are subject to greater wear, such as heels and toes.

Self-patterning yarns

These multicolored yarns are now widely available and produce a variety of effects when knitted, from randomly colored stripes to Fair Isle. A lot of the appeal of self-patterning yarns lies in the fact that you cannot easily predict how each one will look when knitted, which adds to the uniqueness of the socks. Those most widely available tend to be wool-based with additions of fibers such as polyamide, silk, or mohair, which add extra softness or fluffiness to the finished socks. There are also blends of wool with cotton and polyamide, which are perfect for summer socks.

Yarn weights

Each strand of fiber used to make yarn is called a ply, and different types of yarn are made from different numbers of plies. The type of fiber, number of plies, and method of spinning all affect the thickness and weight of the finished yarn. Traditionally, there were standard thicknesses of yarn, such as sport and bulky, but nowadays there are so many different blends and fancy yarns available that these terms may be used for different weights of yarn from one yarn spinner to another. The best thing to do if you are unsure of the weight is to check the ball band to see what size needle to use (see page 16).

The weights of yarn used in this book are:

Light Very fine yarn usually knitted on size 1–3 (2.25–3.25 mm) needles.

Sport About one-and-a-half times the thickness of light-weight yarn, usually knitted on size 3–5 (3.25–3.75 mm) needles.

DK Double-knitting yarn is just under twice the thickness of light-weight yarn, usually knitted on size 5–7 (3.75–4.5 mm) needles.

Bulky This can be anything thicker than DK and may be knitted on size 10 (6 mm) needles upward.

**SELF-PATTERNING
SOCK YARNS FOR
STRIPE EFFECTS**

**MERINO WOOL/
MICROFIBER/CASHMERE
BLEND**

Ball bands

Whether it comes in ball or hank form, the yarn you buy will have a band around it that lists a lot of useful information.

1 Company brand and yarn name.

2 Weight and length—This gives the weight of the ball in ounces or grams and length of the yarn in yards or meters. This information is useful for calculating the total length needed to complete a project. You can then compare alternative yarns to see whether more or fewer balls are needed to match the required length.

3 Fiber content.

4 Shade number and dye lot—The shade number is the manufacturer's reference to a particular color; the dye lot number refers to a specific batch of yarn dyed in that color at the same time. The lot number will change from batch to batch. When knitting a project, it is important to buy sufficient yarn from the same dye lot because these can vary slightly in color. If you are not certain how many balls you will need, it is always best to buy one extra. Where possible, keep ball bands or make a note of dye lots for reference.

5 Needle size—This gives a generally recommended needle size to use. The pattern instructions for your project will tell you which specific size to use. Sometimes a pattern will specify a different needle size from that recommended on the ball band in order to achieve a certain look.

6 Gauge—This is the standard number of stitches and rows measured over 4 in. (10 cm) using the recommended needle size and stockinette stitch. However, check the pattern because the designer may have something else in mind.

7 Washing instructions—These tell you how to wash and take care of the yarn once knitted.

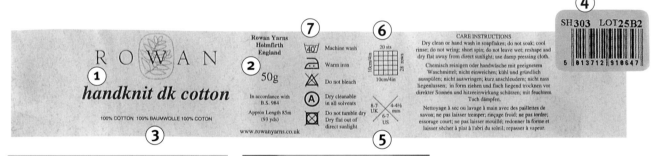

TIP: CHOOSING A DIFFERENT YARN

If you cannot find the specific yarn used in a project, or you would simply prefer to use a different yarn, look at the recommended needle size and gauge provided on the ball band of the yarn that was used in this book (see pages 126–127). Choose a substitute yarn that matches these as closely as possible, but be aware that the number of balls required may be different. Calculate the total length of yarn needed to complete the project by multiplying the number of balls by the length of yarn per ball (you will find this information at the beginning of each project). Then divide the total length of yarn required by the length per ball of the substitute yarn. This will give the number of substitute balls required.

Other materials

Apart from yarn, the only other materials used in the projects in this book are beads (projects 7, 11, and 17), zippers (project 5), and ribbon (project 12). Make sure that any beads you use will stand up to the frequent washing that socks require and are the appropriate size for the yarn being used. If you add beaded embellishments to any additional socks, remember to keep them away from areas that will make the socks uncomfortable to wear, such as soles, heels, and toes. Nylon or plastic zippers are better than metal because they can withstand frequent washing. Ribbon should be soft enough to drape when tied. If the only type you can find to match the color of the yarn is wire-edged, remove the wire before use.

Holding the yarn and needles

It is important to hold the needles and yarn correctly. There are numerous ways of doing this, but the best method is the one that feels most comfortable to you. Choose a medium-weight yarn such as DK to practice with.

Holding the yarn

Both these methods leave your fingertips free to control the needles and tension the yarn so that it pulls quite tight as it passes through your hands.

Holding the needles

Needles can be held from above, in the "knife hold," or from beneath, in the "pen hold." The left needle is always held from above, while the right needle can be held either way.

Scottish method

With this method, both needles are held from above in the knife hold. The left hand controls the needles, moving the stitches toward the tip of the left needle to be worked and guiding the right needle into and out of the stitches. The right needle is supported under the right arm, while the right hand controls the feed of the yarn.

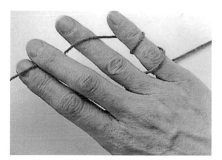

Right hand

Wrap the yarn around the little finger, then snake it over the ring finger, under the middle finger, and over the index finger.

American method

With this method, both needles are held from above in the knife hold. The right hand controls the yarn and moves the right needle into and out of the stitches on the left needle, while the left hand moves the stitches on the left needle.

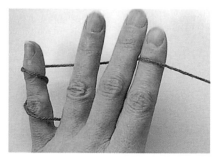

Left hand

Holding the yarn in this hand is faster because the yarn does not have as far to travel to work each stitch. Wrap the yarn around the little finger, then snake it around the other fingers in a way that feels comfortable.

Continental or German method

This is the fastest method of knitting. Both the needles are held from above in the knife hold. The left hand controls the yarn and moves the stitches on the left needle, while the right hand moves the right needle into and out of the stitches on the left needle.

French method

This style of knitting is elegant but more time-consuming. The left needle is held from above in the knife hold, while the right needle is held from beneath in the pen hold between the thumb and index finger. The right index finger is used to guide the yarn around the needles.

Casting on

All knitting starts with a foundation row called a cast-on and this begins with a slipknot. There are various ways of casting on, some of which are best suited to certain stitches, but generally it is a matter of personal preference.

Making a slipknot

Make a slipknot and place it on the left needle to form the first cast-on stitch.

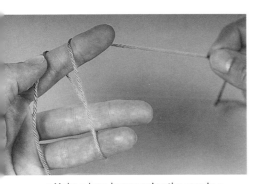

1 Make a loop by wrapping the yarn in a clockwise direction around the first three fingers of your left hand.

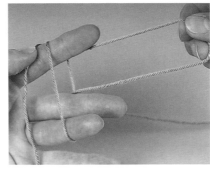

2 Pass the yarn held in your right hand under this loop to form another loop.

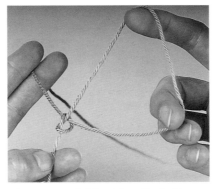

3 Remove your left hand from the first loop and pull the ends to tighten.

4 Place the loop from your right hand onto the needle and tighten. Do not pull too tight.

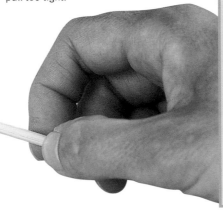

Cable cast-on

This popular cast-on method uses two needles and creates a firm but elastic edge that is suitable for most purposes.

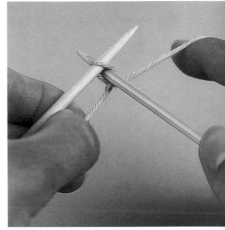

1 Make a slipknot and place it on the left needle. Insert the tip of the right needle into the slipknot from front to back underneath the left needle.

TIP: CORRECTING A TIGHT OR LOOSE CAST-ON

If your cable cast-on is too tight, control this by inserting the right needle between the first two stitches on the left needle before you tighten the yarn of the previous stitch. The needle circumference held between the stitches before tightening the yarn each time will help prevent the cast-on from becoming too tight. Or, try casting on with a larger needle (this applies to both cast-on methods). If your cast-on is too loose, try casting on with a smaller needle. When knitting the first row after casting on, knitting into the back of the stitches can help tighten up the cast-on edge.

Long-tail cast-on

This method is also known as the continental, German, or double cable method. It creates a more elastic edge than the cable cast-on.

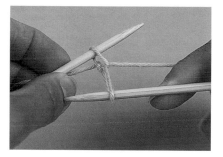

2 Wrap the yarn counterclockwise around the tip of the right needle. Pull the right needle back through the slipknot, drawing the yarn through the slipknot to make a new stitch.

1 Place a slipknot on the needle, leaving a long tail, and hold the needle in your right hand. Wrap the long tail around your left thumb and the yarn coming from the ball over your right forefinger. Slide the needle up through the loop on your thumb.

3 Pull the yarn wrapped around the needle tight, then draw it through the loop on your thumb. Remove your thumb from the loop and pull the cast-on stitch to tighten.

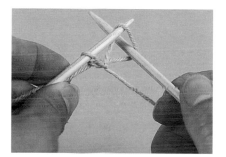

3 Transfer this stitch from the right needle to the left. Gently pull the long end of the yarn (the working yarn) to tighten the stitch around the needle.

2 Wrap the yarn held with your right forefinger clockwise around the needle.

4 Repeat to cast on as many stitches as required.

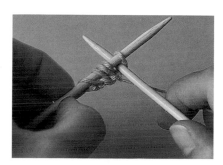

4 Use the same process to make as many stitches as required, but from now on insert the tip of the right needle between the top two stitches on the left needle. Transfer each new stitch to the left needle as before.

TIP: CALCULATING TAIL LENGTH FOR LONG-TAIL CAST-ON

To calculate how long the tail end of yarn needs to be when using the long-tail cast-on method, measure out the yarn to three times the width of the cast-on needed. So, for example, if the width of the knitted piece is to be 4 in. (10 cm), you will need 12 in. (30 cm) of yarn. This also applies if you are nearing the end of a ball of yarn and are not sure whether there is enough to complete a row.

Examples of cable cast-on (top) and long-tail cast-on (below). Both produce edges that are suitable for making socks.

Knit and purl

All knitted fabrics, no matter how complicated or simple, are based on two stitches: knit and purl. Always hold the yarn at the back of the work for a knit stitch and at the front of the work for a purl stitch unless instructed otherwise in the pattern. You can hold the yarn in either your right or left hand to work these stitches.

Knit stitch

Cast on the required number of stitches and hold the yarn at the back of the work. As you work across a row, the stitches will move from the left to the right needle. At the end, swap the needles to work the next row.

Yarn in right hand

1 Insert the tip of the right needle into the stitch on the left needle from front to back underneath the left needle.

2 Use your right forefinger to wrap the yarn counterclockwise around the tip of the right needle.

3 Use the right needle to pull the wrapped yarn through the stitch on the left needle to create a new stitch on the right needle. Slip the original stitch off the left needle.

Yarn in left hand

Insert the tip of the right needle into the stitch on the left needle from front to back underneath the left needle. Using your left forefinger, wrap the yarn counterclockwise around the tip of the right needle. Use the right needle to pull the wrapped yarn through the stitch on the left needle to create a new stitch on the right needle. Slip the original stitch off the left needle.

Purl stitch

Cast on the required number of stitches and hold the yarn at the front of the work. As with knit stitch, swap the needles when you reach the end of the row.

Yarn in right hand

Insert the right needle into the stitch on the left needle from back to front underneath the left needle. Wrap the yarn counterclockwise around the right needle. Use the right needle to pull the wrapped yarn through the stitch on the left needle, then slip the original stitch off the left needle.

Yarn in left hand

Hold the yarn at the front of the work under your left thumb. Insert the right needle into the stitch on the left needle from right to left. Using your left thumb, wrap the yarn counterclockwise around the tip of the right needle. Use the right needle to pull the wrapped yarn through the stitch on the left needle, then slip the original stitch off the left needle.

Stitch patterns

By combining knit and purl stitches in different ways, you can create a variety of textured fabrics. The most frequently used are garter stitch, stockinette stitch, reverse stockinette stitch, seed stitch, and rib.

Garter stitch

Garter stitch is the simplest stitch pattern because it is created by either knitting or purling all the stitches on every row. The fabric it produces is springy and dense in texture and when pressed remains flat. This makes it ideal for use on edges.

Reverse stockinette stitch

This is the same as stockinette stitch but uses the ridged purl side as the right side of the fabric.

Stockinette stitch

Stockinette stitch is the most well-known stitch pattern and is created by alternating knit and purl rows. This produces a more noticeable difference between the front or knit side, which is smooth, and the back or purl side, which has a more ridged appearance.

Seed stitch

This is created by alternating knit and purl stitches on each row, with stitches that are knitted on right side rows also being knitted on wrong side rows, and the same with purl stitches. The fabric created is firm in texture like garter stitch and remains flat after blocking and steaming.

Rib

This stitch makes a very elastic fabric that is mainly used for neckbands and edges. It is worked by alternating knit and purl stitches along each row to produce vertical lines of stitches on both sides of the work. The two most common ribs are single rib and double rib.

Single rib
Work k1, p1 all across each row.

Double rib
Work k2, p2 all across each row.

Binding off

Once you have finished your knitting, you need to secure the stitches by binding them off. Binding off is also used to finish a group of stitches to shape the work. The bound-off edge should stretch about as much as the rest of the knitting.

Binding off knitwise

Throughout the projects, you will be instructed to bind off knitwise, purlwise, or in pattern.

1 Knit the first two stitches from the left needle onto the right needle in the usual way.

2 *With the yarn at the back of the work, insert the tip of the left needle into the first of these knitted stitches, from left to right. Lift this stitch over the second stitch and slip it off the right needle so that you have only one stitch on the right needle.

3 Knit the next stitch on the left needle so that there are two stitches on the right needle once again. Repeat from * until you reach the last stitch. Break off the yarn, leaving a tail of about 6 in. (15 cm).

4 Slip the final stitch off the right needle, thread the tail of yarn through it, and pull tight to secure.

Binding off purlwise

This method follows the same basic procedure as binding off knitwise.

1 Purl the first two stitches from the left needle onto the right needle in the usual way.

2 *With the yarn at the front of the work, insert the tip of the left needle into the first of these knitted stitches, from left to right. Lift this stitch over the second stitch and slip it off the right needle so that you have only one stitch on the right needle.

TIP: COUNTING THE BIND-OFF

When binding off a certain number of stitches, such as for shaping a bootee, count the stitches as you lift them off the needle, not as you work them. The stitch remaining on the right needle does not count as a bound-off stitch.

3 Purl the next stitch on the left needle so that there are two stitches on the right needle once again. Repeat from * until you reach the last stitch. Break off the yarn, leaving a tail of about 6 in. (15 cm).

4 Slip the final stitch off the right needle, thread the tail of yarn through it, and pull tight to secure.

Binding off in pattern

This simply means that you should bind off all knit stitches knitwise and all purl stitches purlwise. For example, if the pattern is double rib, bind off two stitches knitwise, then two stitches purlwise, and so on.

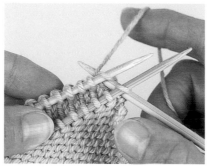

Binding off two sets of stitches together

Binding off two sets of stitches together creates an invisible seam if the two sets of stitches are bound off with right sides facing, or can be made into a decorative feature when the stitches are bound off with wrong sides facing.

1 If you are joining two separate pieces of knitting together, place both needles in your left hand with the appropriate sides of the work facing each other. If you need to join two halves of a single piece of knitting together—such as a toe seam—work as instructed in the pattern, then divide the stitches onto two needles so that the appropriate sides of the fabric are facing and both needles are in your left hand.

2 Insert the tip of a third needle through the first stitch on both needles in your left hand. Work these two stitches together.

3 Work the next pair of stitches together, then use one of the needles in your left hand to lift the first stitch over the second stitch on the right needle, letting it drop off the end of the right needle. When you reach the last pair of stitches, break off the yarn, pull the end of the yarn through both stitches, and tighten.

TIP: NEATENING THE LAST STITCH
The last bind-off stitch is sometimes considerably larger than the others. If you cannot neaten it by sewing it into a seam later, bind off all the stitches except the last one. Slip this stitch onto the right needle. Use the left needle to pick up the final stitch on the row below, then return the slipped stitch to the left needle. Work these two stitches together.

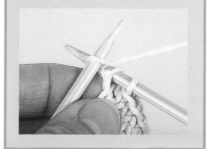

Grafting

Rather than binding off the stitches at the toe of a sock, you can graft them together. Also known as weaving or Kitchener stitch, this creates a virtually invisible seam. Use the standard technique for DK and heavier weight yarns; grafting with a chimney is easier when working with fine yarns.

Standard grafting

1 Thread a yarn needle with yarn and hold both sets of stitches on the knitting needles parallel. Starting at the right-hand edge, insert the yarn needle knitwise (from front to back) through the first stitch on the front knitting needle. Slip this and all remaining stitches off the knitting needles after you pick them up on the yarn needle.

2 Bring the yarn needle purlwise (from back to front) through the second stitch on the front knitting needle.

3 Take the yarn needle behind both sets of stitches and insert purlwise through the first stitch on the back knitting needle.

4 Insert the yarn needle knitwise through the second stitch on the back knitting needle. Continue working in this way across all the stitches on both knitting needles, slipping the stitches off the needles as you go along. Fasten off in the usual way.

Grafting with a chimney

1 Complete the main pattern instructions but do not bind off. Join a contrasting colored yarn of the same weight as the main yarn and use this to work about 1¼ in. (3 cm) of stockinette stitch; this is the chimney. Either bind off the chimney or simply slip the stitches off the needles.

2 Fold the chimney down inside the sock and find the two stitches in the center of the front section. Thread a yarn needle with the main yarn and, working from right to left, insert the needle underneath the left leg of the first stitch and the right leg of the second stitch. Bring half the length of yarn through to the front.

3 Repeat this process on the two central stitches on the back section.

4 Pull the yarn to close the seam, then continue grafting the stitches together in this way. When you reach the left side of the toe, turn the sock around, rethread the needle with the other end of the grafting yarn, and graft the right side of the toe. When all the stitches are secure, unravel and remove the chimney and fasten off the yarn ends in the usual way.

Gauge

Most knitting patterns specify an ideal gauge, which is the number of stitches and rows counted over a certain measurement, usually 4 in. (10 cm) square, worked in a specified stitch pattern and needle size. If you do not work to the correct gauge, the knitting will end up the wrong size.

TIP: A FEW STITCHES CAN MAKE A BIG DIFFERENCE

You may feel that knitting a test swatch is a waste of time but it could well save you from reknitting or abandoning a project or being disappointed with the end result. Knitting is an individual craft—we do not all knit to the same gauge. Although a difference of two or three stitches may seem minor, it could make the difference between a pair of socks feeling fantastic to wear or being an unsatisfactory fit. Accurate gauge is even more important with larger garments. For example, if the gauge should be 20 stitches and yours is 22 stitches to 4 in. (10 cm), a garment measuring 24 in. (60 cm) has six lots of 4 in. (10 cm), so it will be off by 12 stitches. This means your garment will only measure approximately 22 in. (55 cm) and could be too small.

Making a test swatch

It is always advisable to knit a small swatch to measure your gauge and compare it to that stated in the pattern. The instructions will indicate the recommended needle size and what type of stitch pattern the gauge has been measured over.

Using the recommended needle size, cast on the number of stitches specified in the gauge guide plus four more. If the stitches are to be measured over a pattern, cast on the correct multiple of stitches to knit the pattern. Work in the required pattern until the swatch measures approximately 5 in. (12.5 cm) square. Cut the yarn, thread it through the stitches, and slip them off the needle. Do not pull the yarn tight or bind off because this may distort the stitches. Measure the gauge as follows.

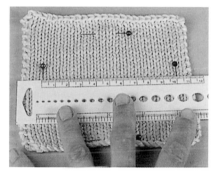

1 Lay the swatch on a flat surface. Placing a ruler in the center of the swatch, measure 4 in. (10 cm) horizontally and vertically across the knitting. Mark each of these distances with two pins.

2 Use the tip of a knitting needle to count the number of stitches and rows between the pins, including half stitches.

Adjusting your gauge

If you have fewer stitches than stated in the gauge guide, your knitting is too loose and the project will be too big. Knit another swatch using smaller needles. If you have more stitches than stated in the gauge guide, your knitting is too tight and the project will be too small. Knit another swatch using larger needles. This should give you the correct gauge if you are off by only one or two stitches. However, if the difference is greater, you may need to adjust the size of item that you make.

Too tight

Correct gauge

Too loose

Patterns and charts

The instructions for knitting a project may be provided in either written or chart form. Always read the whole pattern before you start knitting to ensure that you have everything you need and understand all the instructions.

Essential information

All patterns provide a list containing the size of the finished item, the materials and needles required, the gauge of the piece, and the abbreviations used in the instructions. Although many abbreviations are standardized, such as k for knit and p for purl, some of them vary, so always read the abbreviations in each pattern before you start knitting.

Abbreviations

Abbreviations are used to save space and make written patterns easier to follow. The abbreviations used in this book are:

bead 1	place 1 bead at front of knitting and then slip 1 stitch purlwise
dpn(s)	double-pointed needle(s)
k	knit
k1f&b	knit into front and back of same stitch
m1k	make 1 stitch by picking up horizontal bar before next stitch and knitting into back of it
m1p	make 1 stitch by picking up horizontal bar before next stitch and purling into back of it
p	purl
p1b	purl 1 stitch together with stitch in row below
p1f&b	purl into front and back of same stitch
RS	right side
skpo	slip 1 stitch, knit 1 stitch, pass slip stitch over
sl	slip specified number of stitches knitwise or purlwise as instructed
ssk	slip 1 stitch, slip 1 stitch, knit both stitches on right needle by inserting tip of left needle through front of both loops
st(s)	stitch(es)
tbl	through back of loop
tog	together
WS	wrong side
yb	take yarn between needles to back of work as if to knit
yf	bring yarn between needles to front of work as if to purl
yo	yarn over

Project 19 uses a repeated four-color, slip-stitch stripe design to create socks that look like they are knitted in a Fair Isle pattern.

Repeats

When following the pattern instructions, you will find that some of them appear within curved parentheses and some are marked with an asterisk. Instructions that appear within parentheses are to be repeated. For example, instead of writing "p2, k2, p2, k2," the pattern will simply say "(p2, k2) twice." Asterisks (*) indicate the point to which you should return when you reach the phrase "repeat from *." They may also mark whole sets of instructions that are to be repeated. For example, "repeat from * to **" means repeat the instructions between the single and double asterisks.

Sizing

Some of the sock patterns are written for more than one size; in this book the smallest size is shown first, with subsequent sizes in brackets—for example, small [medium, large]. This format is repeated throughout a pattern for all the sets of figures that differ from one size to the next—for example, the number of stitches to cast on. Follow the instructions for the size you are making. Where only one figure is given, this applies to all sizes. Some of the patterns in this book have separate instructions for each size in order to make them easier for beginners.

TIP: HIGHLIGHT YOUR SIZE

If you are new to working from patterns that have instructions for different sizes in brackets, you may find it easier to follow if you highlight the relevant instructions for the particular size you are making.

Project 7 is easy to knit by following the color design on the chart.

Project 5 is designed in four different sizes, so that you can make a pair for an adult man and woman, as well as two sizes suitable for children of different ages.

Charts

Charts are a graphic representation of your knitting, with each square representing one stitch and each horizontal line representing one row. All charts have a key nearby to explain each of the symbols and/or colors used. Charts have several advantages over row-by-row written instructions: you can see where you are at a glance; you learn to plan ahead, especially in color knitting; and they help to increase your understanding of knitting. Always remember that charts are read from the bottom up. Right side (RS) rows are read from right to left; wrong side (WS) rows are read from left to right. The chart indicates how the work appears on the right side.

Charts are ideal when knitting items with multiple colors, such as the beaded Argyle socks (project 7, above), because you can see at a glance where color changes need to occur.

KEY

☐ Yarn **A**	⊡ P on RS, k on WS
☐ Yarn **B**	
☐ Yarn **C**	◯ Bead 1
☐ K on RS, p on WS	▽ Swiss darn

27

Shaping

There are lots of different ways of increasing or decreasing the number of stitches in order to shape a piece of knitting. The method you use will depend on the number of stitches that need to be increased or decreased, and where in the pattern the shaping is required.

Increasing

The projects in this book use several methods to increase 1 stitch at a time (k1f&b, p1f&b, m1k, m1p), plus the cable increase for increasing multiple stitches.

K1f&b

Work to the point in the row where you need to increase. Knit into the front of the stitch on the left needle in the usual way, but do not slip it off the left needle when you have finished. Keeping the original stitch on the left needle and the yarn at the back of the work, knit into the back of the stitch—you have now increased one stitch. Slip the stitch from the left needle.

TIP: WORK ONE STITCH IN
Work increases and decreases one stitch in from the edges of the fabric to create a neater edge and make sewing seams and picking up stitches easier and neater.

P1f&b

Work this in the same way as k1f&b, but purl into the front and back of the stitch instead of knitting into it, with the yarn at the front of the work.

M1k

This increase uses the horizontal bar that lies between pairs of stitches to make a new stitch. It can be worked anywhere on a row and creates an invisible increase. The pattern will specify whether to make the stitch knitwise or purlwise.

1 Work to the point where you need to increase. Insert the tip of the right needle underneath the horizontal bar lying between the last stitch on the right needle and the first stitch on the left needle.

2 Lift this bar and slip it onto the left needle. Knit into the back of this loop to create a new stitch, slipping the lifted loop off the left needle when you have finished.

M1p

Repeat steps 1 and 2 of m1k, but purl into the back of the lifted loop instead of knitting into it.

Cable increase

It is sometimes necessary to increase multiple stitches. Insert the right needle between the top two stitches on the left needle, then cast on the number of stitches specified in the pattern using the cable cast-on technique.

Decreasing

The projects use several methods of decreasing stitches. Note that the techniques for working two stitches together (k2tog, k2tog tbl, p2tog, p2tog tbl) can also be used to work more than two stitches together in order to decrease a greater number of stitches.

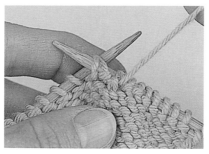

P2tog

Purl 2 together creates a slope to the right on the face of the fabric. Work as for k2tog, but purl the stitches together instead of knitting them.

Skpo

Slip 1, knit 1, pass slip stitch over is a method of decreasing that is often used when making lace holes. It creates a slope to the left on the face of the fabric. Slip one stitch knitwise from the left to the right needle without working it. Knit the next stitch on the left needle in the usual way, then use the left needle to lift the slip stitch over the knit stitch and drop it off the right needle.

K2tog

Knit 2 together creates a slope to the right on the face of the fabric. Work to where you need to decrease, then insert the right needle knitwise into the front of the first two stitches on the left needle. Knit the stitches together as if they were a single stitch. You have now decreased one stitch.

P2tog tbl

Purl 2 together through the back of the loop creates a slope to the left on the face of the fabric. Work as for k2tog tbl, but purl the stitches together through the back of the loop instead of knitting them.

K2tog tbl

Knit 2 together through the back of the loop creates a slope to the left on the face of the fabric. Work to where you need to decrease, then insert the right needle knitwise into the back of the first two stitches on the left needle. Knit the stitches together as if they were a single stitch. You have now decreased one stitch.

Ssk

This decrease creates a slope to the left on the face of the fabric. Slip two stitches knitwise, one at a time, from the left to the right needle. Insert the left needle through the front loop of both stitches, then knit them together from this position.

Bind-off decrease

This decrease is usually done at the beginning of a row. Simply work to where you need to decrease, then bind off the number of stitches specified in the pattern in the usual way. If you are instructed to do it in the middle of a row, you will need to rejoin the yarn to the stitches before the bind-off in order to continue working them.

Circular knitting

Circular knitting, also known as knitting in the round, is a method of knitting that creates a seamless fabric that is ideal for socks. You can knit in the round using double-pointed needles (dpns) or a circular needle.

Using dpns

Double-pointed needles are usually available in sets of four. The stitches are divided onto three of the needles, and the fourth needle is used to work the stitches. Try to space out the stitches a little more than usual when you cast on using dpns; if you cast on too tightly, you may find it difficult to get the sock on. Although stitches are divided over three dpns, you will only ever be knitting with two dpns at a time.

2 Taking care not to twist the stitches, point the first and third dpns toward each other to form a triangle.

Purling

Purling stitches works on exactly the same principle as knitting, but with the yarn held at the front of the work in the usual way. When you have purled across all the stitches on the left dpn, transfer the empty needle to your right hand, move the dpn holding the stitches to be worked next into your left hand, and work the stitches as instructed.

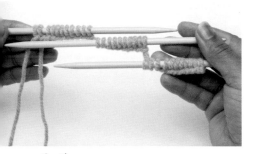

Casting on

1 Cast on the required number of stitches in the usual way. Arrange the stitches evenly onto three dpns.

TIP: FORMING A RING

A good tip for beginners is to cast on the specified number of stitches plus one extra. Divide onto three dpns in the usual way, then knit the last stitch from the third dpn together with the first stitch from the first dpn so that the stitches are joined into a ring, making the needles easier to handle.

Knitting

Hold the yarn at the back of the work and the empty dpn in your right hand. Insert the tip of the empty dpn knitwise into the stitch on the first dpn in your left hand. Knit the stitch in the usual way. When you have knitted across all the stitches on the left dpn, transfer the empty needle to your right hand, move the dpn holding the stitches to be worked next into your left hand, and work across the stitches as instructed. To eliminate the ladders that can appear between each set of stitches on dpns, pull the yarn a little tighter than normal when working the first stitch on the following dpn.

TIP: WEAVING IN A LONG-TAIL CAST-ON

If you have cast on using the long-tail method, a neat way of weaving the tail into the cast-on edge is to work the first few stitches of the first row or round using both the working end of the yarn and the long tail together. This will save you from having to weave it in after the knitting is completed. You can use this technique when working with straight or circular needles, as well as dpns.

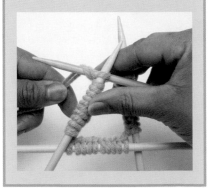

Magic loop technique

This technique allows you to knit a seamless tube using a circular needle. It takes a bit of getting used to but is well worth persevering because it reduces the occurrence of gaps in the finished sock, which can happen when using dpns.

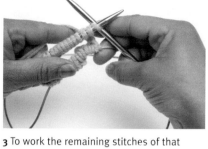

Knitting

1 In order to start knitting, pull the right needle upward until the stitches slide off the tip and down onto the cord. When you begin to knit in rounds, the stitches on the left needle will always be worked off the needle tip and those on the right will stay on the cord.

3 To work the remaining stitches of that round, pull the cord toward you until the stitches on the cord slide up onto the left needle tip. Pull the right needle tip upward so that the stitches you have just worked in the first half of the round slide from the needle down onto the cord. Knit the remaining stitches of the round as normal.

Casting on

1 Cast on the required number of stitches, then slide the stitches down toward the nylon cord. Find the midway point and pull the cord toward you between the two center stitches.

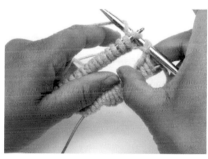

2 With the yarn at the back of the work, insert the right needle tip from front to back into the stitch on the left needle and knit as normal across all the stitches on the left needle.

4 Continue working rounds in this way, sliding the stitches from needle to cord, and cord to needle, as necessary.

2 Holding both sets of stitches between the thumb and fingers of one hand, keep pulling on the cord with your other hand until the stitches slide up onto the tips of both needles. Hold the needles so that the tips point upward and the cord points down, making sure that the stitches attached to the yarn are on the needle tip in your right hand. Also make sure that the stitches are not twisted; the cast-on edge should form a U shape on the inside.

TIP: SLIDING STITCHES

Use a high-quality circular needle that is at least 32 in. (80 cm) long because the longer the needle, the easier it is to slide the stitches up and down as needed. If necessary, pull a bit more tightly than normal when working from one set of stitches to another to avoid creating any gaps.

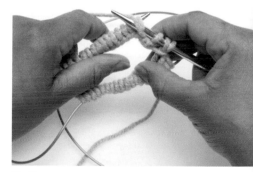

Purling

Purling stitches works on exactly the same principle as knitting, but with the yarn held at the front of the work in the usual way.

Other stitch techniques

Having learned the basics of knitting, purling, and shaping, you will find that there are many variations on these instructions used in knitting patterns to create specific effects.

Slipping stitches

Many techniques involve slipping stitches from one needle to another without working them.

Joining new yarn

Whenever a ball of yarn is about to run out, join a new one at the beginning of a row. When possible, avoid joining a new ball of yarn in the middle of a row.

1 To help keep good tension when starting a new yarn, tie it around the original yarn. Without breaking or cutting the yarn used for the previous row, tie the new yarn around the end of the old yarn, leaving a 6 in. (15 cm) tail.

Carrying yarns up side

When knitting stripes of color, you can break off and join the yarns for each stripe, or carry them up the side of the work. Avoid pulling the yarns too tightly when carrying them up the side because this can cause the edge to distort.

1 Insert the right needle into the first stitch. Lay the second yarn (orange) across the first yarn (pink) and work the next stitch with the second yarn.

Knitwise

To slip a stitch knitwise, insert the tip of the right needle into the stitch on the left needle as if to knit it. Slip the stitch from the left to the right needle without working into it.

2 Slide the knot up to the next stitch and work the row using the new yarn. Hold the tail of yarn out of the way for the first few stitches, then break or cut the old yarn, leaving a 6 in. (15 cm) tail. When you have finished the piece, untie the knot and weave in the ends of yarn.

2 Catch in the unused yarn (pink) on every other row by lying it across the yarn currently in use (orange) before working the first stitch of the new row.

Purlwise

To slip a stitch purlwise, insert the tip of the right needle into the stitch on the left needle as if to purl it. Slip the stitch from the left to the right needle without working into it.

Yarn overs

This involves taking the yarn over the right needle to create a lace hole. This example shows a yarn over between two knit stitches. Instead of knitting the second stitch with the yarn at the back of the work in the usual way, bring the yarn forward between the needles to the front of the work, then wrap it over the right needle to knit the stitch.

Knitting with beads

Beads must be threaded onto the yarn before casting on. You will need a sewing needle and a scrap of sewing thread.

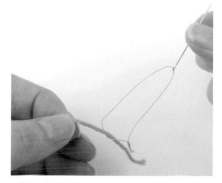

1 Thread a sewing needle that will easily pass through the beads with sewing thread. Knot the ends of the thread, then slip the end of the yarn through the loop of thread.

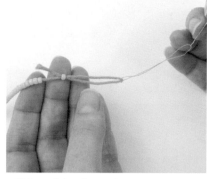

2 Slide each bead onto the needle, then down the thread and onto the yarn. Make sure that you thread them onto the yarn in the correct sequence if necessary.

3 Work to the required position in the pattern and bring the yarn between the needles to the front of the work. Push a bead up the yarn until it is in front of the right needle.

4 Slip the next stitch purlwise from the left to the right needle and bring the bead up to sit in front of the slip stitch. Take the yarn between the needles to the back of the work, then continue the pattern.

Picking up stitches

Picking up and knitting stitches along the edge of a piece of knitting is often used to add an edge or border. The technique is also used along the side of the heel flap in socks in order to work the gusset (shown here).

1 With the right side of the work facing you, insert the left needle from front to back through the first half-stitch in from the edge (picking up a full stitch in from the edge would create too much bulk). On shaped edges, avoid picking up stitches in any large gaps between bound-off stitches or decreases.

2 Use the right needle to knit this picked-up loop in the same way as you would knit a standard stitch. This will create a new stitch on the right needle. Pick up another loop with the left needle and knit it as before. Do this for as many stitches as required, making sure that you space them evenly along the edge.

Constructing a sock

In order to enjoy sock knitting, it helps to understand the basic components that go into creating a sock and how you might be able to make adjustments to the patterns to get a better fit. Don't be afraid to try socks on as you knit them and make any necessary adjustments, such as knitting more rows if you want them to be a little longer.

Project 19 (above) is knitted on two needles, so the heel is "turned" using short-row shaping. The heel of a sock that is knitted in the round (below left) is created by working a heel flap in rows, then "turning" the bottom of the heel flap, and finally resuming working in rounds for the remainder of the sock.

Terminology

It is worth looking at a basic sock and familiarizing yourself with the terminology used to describe its various components.

The foot

This is exactly what it sounds like and is generally worked until it is about 1½ in. (4 cm) shorter than the desired length, to allow some stretch in the sock for a snug fit.

The leg

This usually has an edging at the top, such as rib, and can be long or short, depending on whether you are knitting ankle or knee socks.

The heel

For most people, working the heel is the most daunting part of sock knitting, but it does not need to be. Once you have made your first pair of socks, you will soon learn how straightforward they really are. When knitting a sock on two needles, the heel is constructed by working in short rows. This causes the sock to bend, thereby creating a heel. When working in the round using either double-pointed or circular needles, the heel flap is the only part of the sock that is worked backward and forward in rows. The bottom of the heel is then "turned" from the back of the sock to the bottom using short-row shaping. In most projects, the heels are worked plainly, with attention focused on the stitch pattern in the leg and foot sections—ideal for newcomers to sock knitting.

The gusset

This is the part of the sock that joins the turned heel to the rest of the sock, allowing you to complete the foot. By picking up and knitting stitches down each side of the heel flap and then returning to working in rounds, you incorporate the heel stitches with the stitches being held on the other double-pointed needles or on the cord of the circular needle to create the gusset. This needs to be shaped by decreasing until you arrive at the number of stitches originally cast on.

The toe

This is shaped either by decreasing stitches at both sides of the foot if knitting the sock from the top down, or by increasing stitches if working from the toe up. The toe seam can be finished in various ways, such as grafting or overcasting the seam.

Reinforcing heels

The more socks are enjoyed and worn, the more they are likely to wear out, particularly in areas like the heels. For this reason, it is sometimes necessary to reinforce the heels and there are a number of ways of doing this.

Using a special heel stitch

Some of the projects in this book use techniques like slipping or working into the back of stitches alternated with normally knitted stitches. This "heel stitch" creates a denser fabric that stands up better to frequent wearing and washing. The type of heel stitch varies from project to project.

Using reinforcement yarn

When using yarns not specifically designed for sock knitting that may not be as durable as a special sock yarn, try knitting a wool/synthetic blend yarn in a matching color together with the main yarn just in the heel area to create a harder-wearing fabric there. You can buy reinforcement yarns designed specially for this purpose.

> **TIP: ADJUSTING THE SIZE**
>
> If you are new to knitting socks, it is best to make a couple of pairs to get to grips with how they are constructed before trying to adjust the size. Once you are more confident, you can easily adjust the length of the leg or foot of a sock by working more or fewer rows. Just remember to keep any pattern or shaping correct.
>
> To adjust the circumference of a sock, you need to adjust the number of stitches. Measure around the ankle, just on the joint. Knit a test gauge swatch and multiply the ankle measurement by the number of stitches per inch or centimeter in the gauge swatch. Then round up or down to the nearest whole number. This is the number of stitches you should be working with at that point in the pattern, so adjust accordingly.

Project 13 is knitted on two needles, and the heel worked using short-row shaping.

Project 16 can be knitted on either double-pointed needles or a circular needle. The heel flap is the only part of the sock worked in rows, with the rest being knitted in the round.

Project 18 is knitted on a circular needle, and the heel is reinforced by working it in a twisted slip-stitch pattern.

Project 20 is worked on double-pointed needles, and the heel is reinforced by working it in a slip-stitch and k2tog pattern.

Finishing

Now that you have completed your project, you have come to the task that a lot of knitters hate—weaving in ends, blocking and steaming, and sewing seams. Having knitted a project with such care, take your time. There are many finishing tips and techniques; the ones described here will help you with the projects in this book.

Weaving in ends

All pieces of knitting begin and end with a tail of yarn, and more are created when you join in a new ball, change colors, and sew seams. Always leave a 6 in. (15 cm) tail of yarn, so that it can be threaded into a yarn needle easily and woven into the wrong side of the knitted fabric. Undo any knots joining yarns, then thread the yarn end through a blunt-ended yarn needle.

Along a row

1 Run the needle in and out of the back of stitches of the same color, working along the row for about 4–6 stitches.

Along a seam

Run the needle in and out of the stitches inside the seam at the edge of the knitting for about 3 in. (8 cm). Pull the yarn through and trim the end.

2 Take the needle back, catching in the woven-in yarn for 2–3 stitches. Stretch the knitting widthwise and trim the end of the yarn.

Blocking and steaming

Blocking is the term used for pinning out each knitted piece to the correct size before steaming.

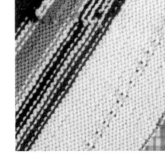

1 Check your pattern for the finished measurements. Using large glass-headed pins and with the wrong side of the knitting facing upward, pin the pieces out to the correct dimensions, taking care not to stretch the knitting out of shape.

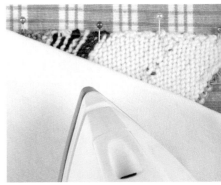

2 Heat an iron to the steam setting, then place a slightly damp towel or thick cloth over the fabric. Holding the iron about 1 in. (2.5 cm) above the surface of the knitting, press the steam button and allow the steam to penetrate the fabric. Do not allow the iron to make contact with the knitted fabric to avoid melting any beads or losing the elasticity in any ribbed or highly textured stitch patterns.

> **TIP: MAKING A BLOCKING BOARD**
> You can use an ironing board for blocking small pieces, or make a blocking board by covering a piece of hardboard with a layer of padding and an over-layer of cotton fabric. Stretch them tight across the board and secure them to the underside with staples, glue, or tape. Choose a checked fabric so that you can use the squares as a guide for pinning out pieces with the edges straight.

Sewing seams

There are several methods of sewing seams together. Overcasting and backstitch are used in this book. Use a blunt-ended yarn needle and matching colored yarn.

Overcasting

This is sometimes referred to as a flat seam because it produces a very narrow seam. Hold the edges of both pieces right sides together in one hand. With your other hand, insert the needle from the back of the work through the edge stitches of both pieces. Pull the yarn through to the front, then take it over the knitted edge and sew once again a few stitches along from where you started. Continue evenly along the edge and secure at both ends by weaving in the yarn ends.

TIP: NEVER SEW SEAMS WITH YARN ENDS

It is better to use a separate piece of yarn to sew seams rather than the tail left over from casting on. If you do make a mistake, it can be easily pulled out of the fabric rather than having to unpick it.

Backstitch

This creates a strong but non-elastic seam and is suitable where firmness is required and for light-weight yarns. It is worked with the wrong sides facing you, so it can be difficult to pattern match exactly. Pin the pieces right sides together, matching the pieces as closely as possible, and keep the stitches near the edge to avoid creating a bulky seam.

1 Secure the seam and yarn by taking the needle twice around the outer edges of the fabric, from back to front.

2 Take the yarn around the outside edge once more, but this time insert the needle through the work from back to front no more than ½ in. (1.3 cm) from where the yarn last came out.

3 Insert the needle from front to back at the point where the first stitch began, then bring the needle back through to the front, the same distance along the edge as before. Repeat this process along the whole seam, then secure the end with a couple of overlapping stitches.

TIP: AFTERCARE

Always refer to the instructions on the yarn ball band for guidelines as to washing or dry cleaning (if you are not going to keep the ball band, make a record of this information in a notebook). Beaded projects should be handwashed with care. Use lukewarm water and a suitable detergent, and try not to agitate the item too much. Avoid wringing because this stretches knitted items out of shape and can damage the beads. Gently squeeze out the excess water by placing the item on a towel and applying light pressure. Felted items, although already shrunk, should be handwashed to avoid additional shrinkage.

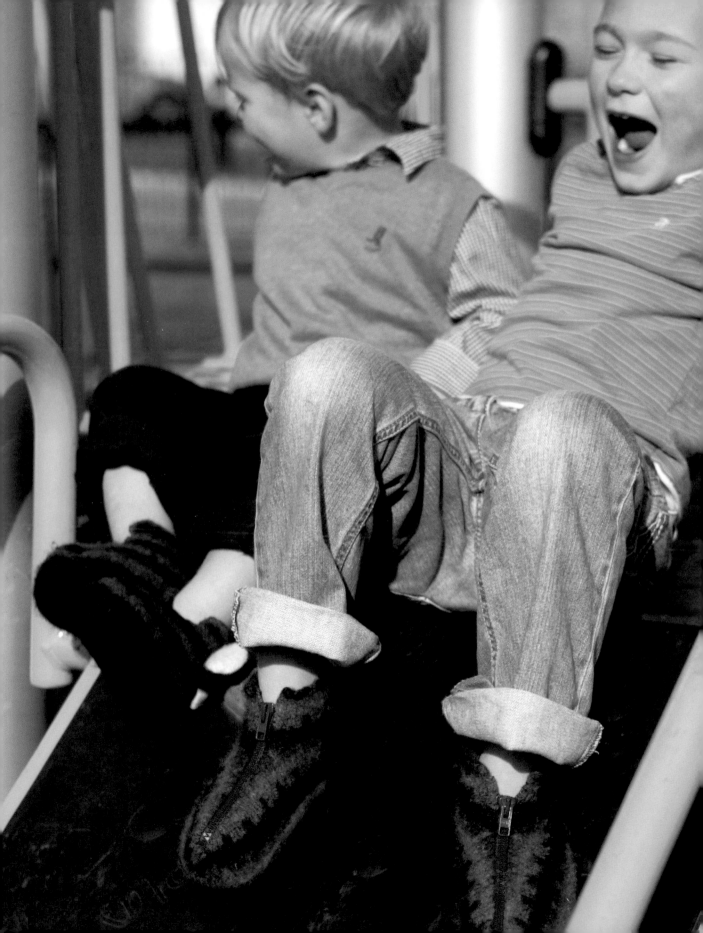

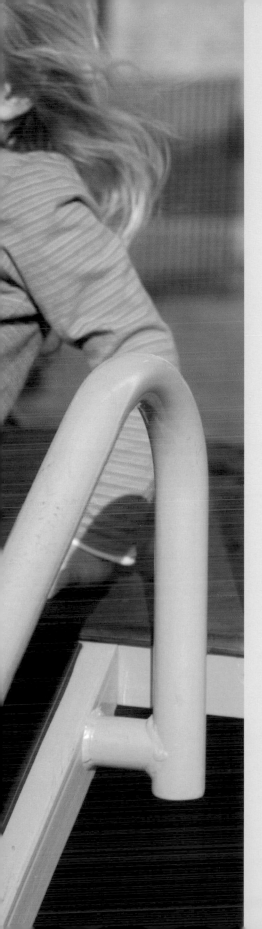

Quick & easy projects

THIS CHAPTER CONTAINS 20 PROJECTS FOR ALL AGES, FROM THE BUTTERFLY AND BUMBLE BOOTS FOR CHILDREN TO THE RIBBON-AND-LACE STOCKINGS AND STRIPY FAIR ISLE SOCKS FOR GROWN-UPS. EACH KNITTER LEARNS AT A DIFFERENT PACE, SO LOOK OUT FOR THE SOCK SYMBOLS TO FIND A PROJECT SUITABLE FOR YOUR CURRENT SKILL LEVEL:

 = EASY

 = AVERAGE

 = MORE CHALLENGING

ALWAYS READ THE ABBREVIATIONS LISTED FOR EACH PATTERN BEFORE YOU START.

PROJECT 1

Textured baby bootees

These bootees are perfect for beginners. The tops are worked in garter stitch and the soles in stockinette stitch to create contrast in texture as well as color. The colors used here would be great for either a baby boy or a girl. For a subtler look that you can make from just one ball of yarn, work the bootees in a single color.

SOLE—1ST SIZE (MAKE 2)

Using size 3 (3.25 mm) needles and yarn A, cast on 7 sts.

Row 1 (RS): Knit.

Row 2: P1, m1p, purl to last st, m1p, p1 (9 sts).

Row 3: Knit.

Row 4: Purl.

Row 5: K1, m1k, knit to last st, m1k, k1 (11 sts).

 SEE STEPS 1–3

Row 6: Purl.

Rows 7–8: Repeat rows 3–4 once.

Row 9: K1, m1k, knit to last st, m1k, k1 (13 sts).

Row 10: Purl.

Rows 11–14: Repeat rows 3–4 twice.

Row 15: K1, m1k, knit to last st, m1k, k1 (15 sts).

Row 16: Purl.

Rows 17–28: Repeat rows 3–4 six times.

Row 29: Knit.

Row 30: P1, p2tog, purl to last 3 sts, p2tog, p1 (13 sts).

Row 31: Knit.

Row 32: P1, p2tog, purl to last 3 sts, p2tog, p1 (11 sts).

Row 33: K1, k2tog, knit to last 3 sts, k2tog, k1 (9 sts).

Row 34: P1, p2tog, purl to last 3 sts, p2tog, p1 (7 sts).

Bind off knitwise.

SOLE—2ND SIZE (MAKE 2)

Using size 3 (3.25 mm) needles and yarn A, cast on 7 sts.

Row 1 (RS): Knit.

Row 2: P1, m1p, purl to last st, m1p, p1 (9 sts).

Row 3: K1, m1k, knit to last st, m1k, k1 (11 sts).

 SEE STEPS 1–3

Row 4: Purl.

Row 5: Knit.

Row 6: Purl.

Row 7: K1, m1k, knit to last st, m1k, k1 (13 sts).

Row 8: Purl.

Row 9: Knit.

Row 10: Purl.

Rows 11–14: Repeat rows 7–10 once (15 sts).

Row 15: K1, m1k, knit to last st, m1k, k1 (17 sts).

Rows 16–30: Beginning with a purl row, work 15 rows in stockinette stitch.

Row 31: K1, k2tog, knit to last 3 sts, k2tog, k1 (15 sts).

Row 32: Purl.

Row 33: K1, k2tog, knit to last 3 sts, k2tog, k1 (13 sts).

Row 34: P1, p2tog, purl to last 3 sts, p2tog, p1 (11 sts).

Row 35: K1, k2tog, knit to last 3 sts, k2tog, k1 (9 sts).

Row 36: P1, p2tog, purl to last 3 sts, p2tog, p1 (7 sts).

Bind off knitwise.

BEFORE YOU START

MEASUREMENTS

1st size

To fit ages 3–6 months

Length from heel to toe: 3¾ in. (9.5 cm)

2nd size

To fit ages 6–9 months

Length from heel to toe: 4 in. (10 cm)

YARN

DK-weight yarn (100% merino wool; approx. 175 yds/160 m per 2 oz/50 g ball) in 2 colors:

A Lime x 1 ball

B Orange x 1 ball

NEEDLES

Size 3 (3.25 mm)

GAUGE

24 sts x 36 rows = 4 in. (10 cm) in stockinette stitch using size 3 (3.25 mm) needles

26 sts x 56 rows = 4 in. (10 cm) in garter stitch using size 3 (3.25 mm) needles

ABBREVIATIONS

k—knit; **m1k**—make 1 stitch knitwise; **m1p**—make 1 stitch purlwise; **p**—purl; **RS**—right side; **st(s)**—stitch(es); **tog**—together; **WS**—wrong side

NOTE: WORKING DIFFERENT SIZES

The instructions for the soles are written separately for each size so that they are easy for a beginner to follow. The instructions for the upper sections are combined, with the first figure referring to the 1st size and the figure in square brackets referring to the 2nd size. Where only one figure is given, this refers to both sizes.

1 Start the sole for both sizes by casting on 7 sts. If you would prefer the soles to be the same color as the uppers, use yarn B (there will be enough yarn in a single ball).

2 Work m1k or m1p by using the right needle to lift the horizontal bar before the next stitch and transfer it onto the left needle.

3 Knit (m1k) or purl (m1p, shown here) into the back of this bar to create a new stitch, then slip the bar off the left needle.

BACK—BOTH SIZES (MAKE 2)

Using size 3 (3.25 mm) needles and yarn B, cast on 5 [6] sts.

Row 1 (RS): Knit.

Row 2: Cast on 5 [5] sts at beginning of row, knit these sts, then knit to end (10 [11] sts).

Row 3: Knit.

Row 4: Cast on 4 [5] sts at beginning of row, knit these sts, then knit to end (14 [16] sts).

 SEE STEP 4

Rows 5–24: Knit.

Row 25: Bind off 5 [6] sts knitwise at beginning of row, then knit to end (9 [10] sts).

 SEE STEP 5

Row 26: Knit.

Row 27: K1, k2tog, knit to end (8 [9] sts).

Row 28: Knit.

Repeat rows 27–28 three [four] times (5 [5] sts).

Knit 4 more rows.

Next row: K1, m1k, knit to end.

Next row: Knit.

Repeat last 2 rows three [four] times (9 [10] sts).

Next row (RS): Cast on 5 [6] sts at beginning of row, knit these sts, then knit to end (14 [16] sts).

Knit another 20 rows.

Next row (WS): Bind off 4 [5] sts knitwise at beginning of row, then knit to end (10 [11] sts).

Next row: Knit.

Next row: Bind off 5 [5] sts knitwise at beginning of row, then knit to end (5 [6] sts).

Next row: Knit.

Bind off remaining sts knitwise.

FRONT—BOTH SIZES (MAKE 2)

Using size 3 (3.25 mm) needles and yarn B, cast on 12 sts.

Row 1 (RS): Knit.

Row 2: Cast on 6 [8] sts at beginning of row, knit these sts, then knit to end (18 [20] sts).

Row 3: As row 2 (24 [28] sts).

Rows 4–18: Knit.

Row 19: K6 [8], k2tog, k8, k2tog, knit to end (22 [26] sts).

Rows 20–22: Knit.

Row 23: K5 [7], k2tog, k8, k2tog, knit to end (20 [24] sts).

Rows 24–26: Knit.

Row 27: K4 [6], k2tog, k8, k2tog, knit to end (18 [22] sts).

Row 28: Knit.

Row 29: K3 [5], k2tog, k8, k2tog, knit to end (16 [20] sts).

Row 30: Knit.

Row 31: K2 [4], k2tog, k1, k2tog, k2, k2tog, k1, k2tog, knit to end (12 [16] sts).

Row 32: Knit.

Row 33 (1st size only): (K2tog) 6 times. Bind off knitwise.

The following instructions are for the 2nd size only:

Row 33: K2, k2tog, k1, k2tog, k2, k2tog, k1, k2tog, k2 (12 sts).

Row 34: Knit.

Row 35: (K2tog, k1) to end (8 sts).

Row 36: Knit.

Bind off knitwise.

4 Start shaping the back piece by casting on extra stitches at the beginning of the 2nd and 4th rows using the cable cast-on method.

5 Start shaping the U-shaped edge where the front piece will go by binding off stitches at the beginning of row 25.

6 To assemble the upper section, place the back piece flat on a table and fold the front piece in half.

SEE ALSO
Blanket stitch, page 47 (step 7)
Chain stitch, page 55
(steps 13–14)

FINISHING

Weave in any loose ends to WS on all pieces, then block and steam the sole only. Place the back piece flat on a table RS up, with the U-shaped edge to the right. Fold the front piece in half lengthwise, WS together and with side seams touching. Place the folded front piece on top of the back piece, with cast-on and U-shaped edges aligned, and fold over bind-off edge of back piece to sandwich front piece between. Overcast the two pieces together along the U-shaped edge.

 See steps 6–8

Fold the whole upper RS together and overcast the cast-on and bind-off edges of the back piece together to create the center back seam.

 See step 9

Turn the upper RS out and position the sole with RS facing outward. Blanket stitch the sole in place using yarn B. Sew a line of chain stitch neatly around the opening edge using yarn A.

7 Fold the back piece around the front piece so that the U-shaped edge of the back piece aligns with the folded edge of the front piece.

8 Overcast the two edges together, working as close to the edges as possible to create a narrow seam.

9 Complete the upper by overcasting the center back seam, again working close to the edges to create a narrow seam.

 **PROJECT 2**

Stripy toddler toasties

These toasties are knitted on two needles and constructed in the same way as the textured baby bootees (project 1), but are designed for an older child. The upper is worked in two brightly contrasting shades of soft merino wool, while the sole is worked in the same garter stitch texture but in a single color. You could easily make the soles striped if you wish, though. Whether you choose to make the toasties in bright or subtle colors, they are fun for you to knit and for little ones to wear.

SOLE (MAKE 2)

Using size 3 (3.25 mm) needles and yarn A, cast on 5 sts.

Row 1 (RS): Knit.

Row 2: K1, m1k, knit to last st, m1k, k1 (7 sts).

Row 3: Knit.

Row 4: As row 2 (9 sts).

Rows 5–7: Knit.

Row 8: As row 2 (11 sts).

Rows 9–13: Knit.

Row 14: As row 2 (13 sts).

Rows 15–21: Knit.

Row 22: As row 2 (15 sts).

Rows 23–31: Knit.

Row 32: As row 2 (17 sts).

Rows 33–57: Knit.

Row 58: K1, k2tog, knit to last 3 sts, k2tog, k1 (15 sts).

Rows 59–61: Knit.

Row 62: As row 58 (13 sts).

Row 63: Knit.

Rows 64–67: Repeat row 58 four times (5 sts).

Bind off knitwise.

BACK (MAKE 2)

Using size 3 (3.25 mm) needles and yarn A, cast on 6 sts. Without breaking off yarn A, join yarn B.

Row 1 (RS): Using yarn B, knit.

Row 2: Knit.

Row 3: Using yarn A, cast on 5 sts at beginning of row, knit these sts, then knit to end (11 sts).

Row 4: Knit using yarn A, weaving in yarn B to take it to the end of the row.

👁 SEE STEPS 1–3

Row 5: Using yarn B, cast on 5 sts at beginning of row, knit these sts, then knit to end (16 sts).

Row 6: Knit using yarn B, weaving in yarn A to take it to the end of the row.

Rows 7–8: Using yarn A, knit.

Rows 9–10: Using yarn B, knit.

Rows 11–30: Work in garter stitch stripes as set by rows 7–10, carrying yarns up side of work and taking care not to pull them too tightly.

👁 SEE STEP 4 OVERLEAF

Row 31: Using yarn A, knit.

Row 32: Bind off 5 sts knitwise at beginning of row, then knit to end (11 sts).

👁 SEE STEP 5 OVERLEAF

BEFORE YOU START

MEASUREMENTS

To fit ages 12–24 months
Length from heel to toe: 4¾ in.
(12 cm)

YARN

DK-weight yarn (100% merino wool; approx. 175 yds/160 m per 2 oz/50 g ball) in 2 colors:

A Blue x 1 ball
B Green x 1 ball

NEEDLES

Size 3 (3.25 mm)

GAUGE

26 sts x 56 rows = 4 in. (10 cm) in garter stitch using size 3 (3.25 mm) needles

ABBREVIATIONS

k—knit; **m1k**—make 1 stitch knitwise; **RS**—right side; **st(s)**—stitch(es); **tog**—together; **WS**—wrong side

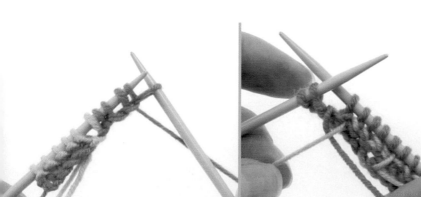

1 Start shaping the back piece by casting on 5 sts at the beginning of row 3 using yarn A. Complete row 3, then knit across row 4 until you reach the cast-on stitches.

2 When completing row 4 using yarn A, you also need to weave in yarn B to take it to the end of row. Do this by picking up yarn B and placing it across the top of yarn A.

3 Pick up yarn A and work the next stitch. Continue weaving the two yarns together in this way before working every stitch so that both yarns move to the end of the row.

Row 33: Using yarn B, knit to last 3 sts, k2tog, k1 (10 sts).

Row 34: K1, k2tog, knit to end (9 sts).

Row 35: Using yarn A, knit.

Row 36: K1, k2tog, knit to end (8 sts).

Row 37: Using yarn B, knit.

Row 38: K1, k2tog, knit to end (7 sts).

Row 39: Using yarn A, knit.

Row 40: K1, k2tog, knit to end (6 sts).

Row 41: Using yarn B, knit.

Row 42: K1, k2tog, knit to end (5 sts).

Rows 43–44: Using yarn A, knit.

Rows 45–46: Using yarn B, knit.

Rows 47–50: Repeat rows 43–46.

Row 51: Using yarn A, knit.

Row 52: K1, m1k, knit to end (6 sts).

Row 53: Using yarn B, knit.

Row 54: K1, m1k, knit to end (7 sts).

Row 55: Using yarn A, knit.

Row 56: K1, m1k, knit to end (8 sts).

Row 57: Using yarn B, knit.

Row 58: K1, m1k, knit to end (9 sts).

Row 59: Using yarn A, knit.

Row 60: K1, m1k, knit to end (10 sts).

Row 61: Using yarn B, knit to last st, m1k, k1 (11 sts).

Row 62: Cast on 5 sts at beginning of row, knit these sts, then knit to end (16 sts).

Rows 63–64: Using yarn A, knit.

Rows 65–66: Using yarn B, knit.

Rows 67–86: Repeat rows 63–66 five times.

Rows 87–88: As rows 63–64.

Row 89: Using yarn B, bind off 5 sts knitwise at beginning of row, weaving in yarn A as you do so, then knit to end using yarn B (11 sts).

 SEE STEP 6

Row 90: Using yarn B, knit. Break off yarn B.

Row 91: Using yarn A, bind off 5 sts knitwise at beginning of row, then knit to end (6 sts).

Row 92: Knit. Bind off knitwise.

FRONT (MAKE 2)

Using size 3 (3.25 mm) needles and yarn A, cast on 12 sts. Without breaking off yarn A, join yarn B.

Row 1 (RS): Using yarn B, knit.

Row 2: Cast on 11 sts at beginning of row, knit these sts, then knit to end (23 sts).

Row 3: Using yarn A, cast on 11 sts at beginning of row, knit these sts, then knit to end (34 sts).

Row 4: Knit using yarn A, weaving in yarn B to take it to the end of the row.

Rows 5–6: Using yarn B, knit.

Rows 7–8: Using yarn A, knit.

Rows 9–28: Work in garter stitch stripes as set by rows 5–8, carrying yarns up side of work and taking care not to pull them too tightly.

Rows 29–30: As rows 5–6.

Row 31: Using yarn A, k10, k2tog, k10, k2tog, knit to end (32 sts).

Row 32: Knit.

Row 33: Using yarn B, k9, k2tog, k10, k2tog, knit to end (30 sts).

Row 34: Knit.

Row 35: Using yarn A, k8, k2tog, k10, k2tog, knit to end (28 sts).

Row 36: Knit.

Row 37: Using yarn B, k3, (k2tog, k2) to last st, k1 (22 sts).

Row 38: Knit.

Rows 39–40: Using yarn A, knit.

Row 41: Using yarn B, k1, k2tog, k1, (k2tog, k2) 3 times, (k2tog, k1) twice (16 sts).

Row 42: Knit.

Row 43: Using yarn A, k1, (k2tog, k2) to last 3 sts, k2tog, k1 (12 sts).

Row 44: Knit. Break off yarn A.

Row 45: Using yarn B, k1, (k2tog, k2) to last 3 sts, k2tog, k1 (9 sts).

Row 46: K2tog to last st, k1. Bind off knitwise.

4 After completing each stripe, don't break off the yarn. Simply drop that color and pick up the new color from under the old one to work the next stripe.

5 Start shaping the U-shaped edge where the front piece will go by binding off 5 sts at the beginning of row 32.

6 On row 89, place yarn A across the top of yarn B before binding off each stitch with yarn B. This will move yarn A to the correct position for working row 91 later.

SEE ALSO
Assembling upper section,
pages 42–43 (steps 6–9)

FINISHING

Weave in any loose ends to WS on all
pieces, then block and steam the sole
only. Place the back piece flat on a table
RS up, with the U-shaped edge to the
right. Fold the front piece in half
lengthwise, WS together and with side
seams touching. Place the folded front
piece on top of the back piece, with
cast-on and U-shaped edges aligned,
and fold down bind-off edge of back
piece to sandwich front piece between.
Overcast the two pieces together along
the U-shaped edge. Fold the whole
upper RS together and overcast the
cast-on and bind-off edges of the back
piece together to create the center
back seam. Turn the upper RS out
and position the sole with RS facing
outward. Blanket stitch the sole in
place using yarn A.

 SEE STEP 7

7 To work blanket stitch, take the
needle through the seam, catch the
yarn around the top of it, and pull
through. Continue around the
whole seam.

PROJECT 3

Buttoned baby bootees

These bootees, knitted in a sumptuously soft cashmere blend yarn, make the perfect gift for a baby. Their simple shape and seed stitch texture are combined with a clever construction technique to create a cute rounded shape. Make them in traditional girly pink or boyish blue, or choose any other color you like. The bootees are edged with blanket stitch and finished with a decorative shell button.

SOLE (MAKE 2)

Using size 6 (4 mm) needles and yarn A doubled, cast on 5 sts.

Row 1 (RS): (K1, p1) to last st, k1.

Rows 2–4: (K1, p1) to last st, k1.

Row 5: P1, m1k, p1, k1, p1, m1k, p1 (7 sts).

Row 6: (P1, k1) to last st, p1.

Row 7: K1, m1p, (k1, p1) to end (8 sts).

Row 8: (P1, k1) to end.

Row 9: P1, m1k, (p1, k1) to last st, m1p, k1 (10 sts).

Row 10: (K1, p1) to end.

Row 11: (P1, k1) to end.

Row 12: (K1, p1) to end.

Row 13: K1, m1p, (k1, p1) to last st, k1 (11 sts).

Rows 14–24: (K1, p1) to last st, k1.

Row 25: P2tog, (k1, p1) to last st, k1 (10 sts).

Row 26: P2tog, (k1, p1) to end (9 sts).

Row 27: K2tog, (p1, k1) to last st, p1 (8 sts).

Row 28: K2tog, (p1, k1) twice, p2tog (6 sts).

Row 29: K2tog, (p1, k1) to end (5 sts).

Bind off in pattern.

UPPER (MAKE 2)

Using size 6 (4 mm) needles and yarn A doubled, cast on 7 sts.

Row 1 (RS): (K1, p1) to last st, k1.

Row 2: P1, m1k, (p1, k1) twice, p1, m1k, p1 (9 sts).

Row 3: K1, m1p, (k1, p1) to last 2 sts, k1, m1p, k1 (11 sts).

Row 4: P1, m1k, (p1, k1) to last 2 sts, p1, m1k, p1 (13 sts).

Row 5: K1, m1p, (k1, p1) to last 2 sts, k1, m1p, k1 (15 sts).

Row 6: P1, m1k, (p1, k1) to last 2 sts, p1, m1k, p1 (17 sts).

Row 7: K1, m1p, (k1, p1) to end (18 sts).

Row 8: K1, m1p, (k1, p1) to last st, k1 (19 sts).

Rows 9–16: (K1, p1) to last st, k1.

Row 17: P2tog, (k1, p1) to last st, k1 (18 sts).

Row 18: (K1, p1) to end.

Row 19: K2tog, (p1, k1) to end (17 sts).

Row 20: (K1, p1) to last 3 sts, k1, p2tog (16 sts).

Row 21: K2tog, (p1, k1) to end (15 sts).

Row 22: (K1, p1) to last 3 sts, k1, p2tog (14 sts).

Row 23: Bind off 2 sts at beginning of row in pattern, (k1, p1) to last st, k1 (12 sts).

Row 24: (K1, p1) to last 2 sts, k2tog (11 sts).

Row 25: Bind off 2 sts at beginning of row in pattern, (p1, k1) to end (9 sts).

Rows 26–28: (K1, p1) to last st, k1.

Row 29: P2tog, (k1, p1) to last st, k1 (8 sts).

Row 30: (K1, p1) to end.

Row 31: (P1, k1) to end.

Row 32: (K1, p1) to end.

Row 33: K2tog, (p1, k1) to end (7 sts).

Rows 34–40: (K1, p1) to last st, k1.

Row 41: P1, m1k, (p1, k1) to end (8 sts).

Row 42: (K1, p1) to end.

Row 43: (P1, k1) to end.

Row 44: (K1, p1) to end.

Row 45: K1, m1p, (k1, p1) to last st, k1 (9 sts).

Rows 46–48: (K1, p1) to last st, k1.

Row 49: Bind off 4 sts at beginning of row in pattern, (p1, k1) to end (5 sts).

Row 50: (K1, p1) to end.

Row 51: Bind off 2 sts at beginning of row in pattern, p1, k1 (3 sts).

Row 52: K1, p1, k1.

Bind off remaining 3 sts in pattern.

FINISHING

Weave in any loose ends to WS on all pieces; do not block or steam. Place the upper section flat on a table RS up, with pointed tip to the top left. Using a doubled length of yarn B, work blanket stitch around the edge, stopping at the fullest part on the right-hand side. Fold the upper, with RS facing outward, so that the pointed tip meets the end of the blanket stitching and sew together using a doubled length of yarn A.

 See step 1

Position the sole with RS facing outward and blanket stitch in place using a doubled length of yarn A.

 See step 2

Sew a button behind the blanket stitched seam on the outer side of the bootee, using yarn A or sewing thread.

See step 3

Before you start

MEASUREMENTS
To fit ages 3–6 months
Length from heel to toe: 4½ in. (11.5 cm)

YARN
DK-weight yarn (35% cotton, 25% polyamide, 18% viscose, 9% cashmere; approx. 197 yds/180 m per 2 oz/50 g ball) in 2 colors:
A Pink or blue x 1 ball
B White x short length
Yarn is used doubled throughout

OTHER MATERIALS
Two ³⁄₈ in. (1 cm) shell buttons

NEEDLES
Size 6 (4 mm)

GAUGE
22 sts x 32 rows = 4 in. (10 cm) in seed stitch using size 6 (4 mm) needles and yarn doubled

ABBREVIATIONS
k—knit; **m1k**—make 1 stitch knitwise; **m1p**—make 1 stitch purlwise; **p**—purl; **RS**—right side; **st(s)**—stitch(es); **tog**—together; **WS**—wrong side

1 Fold the upper so that the pointed tip meets the end of the blanket stitching and sew together using yarn A.

2 Blanket stitch the sole in place using a doubled length of yarn A. For each stitch, take the needle through the seam, catch the yarn around the top of it, and pull through.

3 Sew a decorative button behind the blanket stitched seam, making sure that the button is securely attached.

 **PROJECT 4**

Butterfly and bumble boots

These boots are great fun to make and wear. Worked on two needles in simple stripes and then felted, they make a great first shaping and felting project for new knitters. Each of the color schemes—lilac and pink for girls, and black and mustard for boys—is finished with a matching bug.

SOLE (MAKE 2)

Using size 9 (5.5 mm) needles and yarn A, cast on 5 sts.

Row 1 (RS): Knit.

Row 2: Purl.

Row 3: K1, m1k, knit to last st, m1k, k1 (7 sts).

 See step 1

Row 4: Purl.

Row 5: K1, m1k, knit to last st, m1k, k1 (9 sts).

Row 6: Purl.

Rows 7–10: Repeat rows 1–2 twice.

Row 11: K1, m1k, knit to last st, m1k, k1 (11 sts).

Row 12: Purl.

Rows 13–16: Repeat rows 1–2 twice.

Row 17: K1, m1k, knit to last st, m1k, k1 (13 sts).

Row 18: Purl.

Rows 19–30: Repeat rows 1–2 six times.

Row 31: K1, k2tog, knit to last 3 sts, k2tog, k1 (11 sts).

See steps 2–3

Row 32: Purl.

Row 33: Knit.

Row 34: Purl.

Row 35: K1, k2tog, knit to last 3 sts, k2tog, k1 (9 sts).

Row 36: Purl.

Row 37: K1, k2tog, knit to last 3 sts, k2tog, k1 (7 sts).

Row 38: (P1, p2tog) twice, p1 (5 sts).

Bind off knitwise.

BEFORE YOU START

MEASUREMENTS

To fit ages 12–24 months

Length from heel to toe: 4½ in. (11.5 cm)

YARN

DK-weight tweed-effect yarn (100% pure new wool; approx. 123 yds/113 m per 2 oz/50 g ball) in 3 colors:

Butterfly boots

A Pink x 1 ball

B Lilac x 1 ball

C Mustard x small amount for embroidery

Bumble boots

A Black x 1 ball

B Mustard x 1 balll

C White x small amount for bug

NEEDLES

Size 9 (5.5 mm)

GAUGE

21 sts x 32 rows = 4 in. (10 cm) in stockinette stitch stripes using size 9 (5.5 mm) needles after felting (see page 59)

ABBREVIATIONS

k—knit; **k1f&b**—knit into front and back of same stitch; **m1k**—make 1 stitch knitwise; **p**—purl; **p1f&b**—purl into front and back of same stitch; **RS**—right side; **st(s)**—stitch(es); **tbl**—through back of loop; **tog**—together; **WS**—wrong side

1 Start shaping the sole by increasing the number of stitches using m1k. Lift the horizontal bar before the next stitch, place it on the left needle, and knit into the back of it.

2 Decrease the number of stitches at the other end of the sole by knitting the first stitch in row 31, then knitting two stitches together (k2tog).

3 Decrease another stitch using k2tog at the end of row 31 to create symmetrical shaping. Continue decreasing in this way.

UPPER (MAKE 2)

Using size 9 (5.5 mm) needles and yarn A, cast on 62 sts.

Row 1 (RS): Knit.

Row 2: Purl.

Rows 3–4: Repeat rows 1–2 once.

Without breaking off yarn A, join yarn B.

Rows 5–8: Using yarn B, repeat rows 1–4.

Continue the stripe pattern, alternating colors as set by rows 1–8 and carrying the yarns up the side of the work when not in use.

Row 9: Knit.

Row 10: Purl.

Row 11: (K1, k2tog) twice, knit to last 6 sts, (k2tog, k1) twice (58 sts).

Row 12: Purl.

Row 13: (K1, k2tog) twice, knit to last 6 sts, (k2tog, k1) twice (54 sts).

Row 14: (P1, p2tog) twice, purl to last 6 sts, (p2tog, p1) twice (50 sts).

Row 15: (K1, k2tog) twice, knit to last 6 sts, (k2tog, k1) twice (46 sts).

Row 16: (P1, p2tog) twice, purl to last 6 sts, (p2tog, p1) twice (42 sts).

Row 17: (K1, k2tog) twice, knit to last 6 sts, (k2tog, k1) twice (38 sts).

Row 18: Bind off 4 sts purlwise at beginning of row, then purl to end (34 sts).

Row 19: Bind off 4 sts knitwise at beginning of row, then knit to end (30 sts).

Row 20: (P1, p2tog) twice, purl to last 6 sts, (p2tog, p1) twice (26 sts). Place marker at each end of row 20.

Row 21: (K1, k2tog) twice, knit to last 6 sts, (k2tog, k1) twice (22 sts).

Row 22: Purl.

Row 23: Knit.

Row 24: Purl. Break off yarn B.

Rows 25–28: Repeat rows 1–2 twice.

Bind off knitwise using yarn B.

BUTTERFLY WINGS (MAKE 4)

Using size 9 (5.5 mm) needles and yarn A, cast on 6 sts.

Row 1: Knit.

Row 2: K1, m1k, purl to last st, m1k, k1 (8 sts).

Row 3: Knit to last st, m1k, k1 (9 sts).

Row 4: K1, m1k, purl to last st, m1k, k1 (11 sts).

Row 5: Knit to last st, m1k, k1 (12 sts).

Row 6: K1, p3, p2tog, turn.

Work 5 sts on left needle as follows.

Next row: Knit.

Next row: K1, p3, k1.

Next row: K2tog tbl, k1, k2tog (3 sts).

Bind off purlwise.

◉ SEE STEP 4

With WS facing, rejoin yarn to remaining 6 sts and complete wing as follows.

Row 6: K1, purl to last st, m1k, k1 (7 sts).

4 Working on 5 sts only, complete one half of the wing, then bind off in the usual way.

5 Rejoin the yarn to the remaining 6 sts to complete the other half of the wing, binding off securely to finish it.

6 Roll up the body from bind-off to cast-on edge to create a small sausage shape, then sew together using yarn C.

Row 7: Knit.
Row 8: K1, purl to last st, k1.
Row 9: Knit.
Row 10: K2tog, purl to last 2 sts, k2tog tbl (5 sts).
Row 11: K2tog tbl, k1, k2tog (3 sts).
Bind off purlwise.

 SEE STEP 5

Make two wings as instructed above, then make the remaining two wings by substituting knit for purl, and purl for knit, throughout the instructions. You will need one wing made using knit instructions and one using purl instructions for each boot.

BUTTERFLY BODY (MAKE 2)
Using size 9 (5.5 mm) needles and yarn C, cast on 9 sts. Beginning with a knit row, work 7 rows in stockinette stitch. Bind off knitwise.

SEWING THE BUTTERFLY
Weave in any loose ends to WS on all pieces, then block and steam both pairs of wings. Roll the body into a small sausage shape and secure along the edge using yarn C. Create antennae by using yarn C to attach two small tassels to the top of the body, then sew the wings to the body.

 SEE STEPS 6–9

7 For each tassel, cut two 6 in. (15 cm) lengths of yarn C, fold in half, and thread the center through a yarn needle. Insert the needle through the top of the body.

8 Use the needle to pull the loop of yarn through the body. Remove the needle, then insert the ends of yarn through the loop and pull tight. Trim the antennae as desired.

9 Sew the wings to the back seam on the butterfly body using yarn A.

BEE BODY (MAKE 2)

Using size 9 (5.5 mm) needles and yarn A, cast on 4 sts.

Row 1 (RS): Knit.

Row 2: (P1f&b) to end (8 sts).

Row 3: (K1f&b, k1) to end (12 sts).

Row 4: Purl. Without breaking off yarn A, join yarn B.

Row 5: Using yarn B, knit.

Row 6: Purl.

Row 7: Using yarn A, knit.

Row 8: Purl.

Row 9: Using yarn B, knit.

Row 10: Purl. Break off yarn B.

Row 11: Using yarn A, knit.

Row 12: Purl.

Row 13: (K2tog, k2, k2tog) twice (8 sts).

Row 14: (K2tog) 4 times (4 sts).

Bind off knitwise.

BEE WINGS (MAKE 4)

Using size 9 (5.5 mm) needles and yarn C, cast on 4 sts.

Row 1 (RS): Knit.

Row 2: K1, m1k, purl to last st, m1k, k1 (6 sts).

Row 3: K1, m1k, knit to last st, m1k, k1 (8 sts).

Row 4: K1, purl to last st, k1.

Row 5: K1, m1k, knit to last st, m1k, k1 (10 sts).

Row 6: K1, purl to last st, k1.

Row 7: Knit.

Row 8: K1, purl to last st, k1.

Row 9: K2tog tbl, knit to last 2 sts, k2tog (8 sts).

Row 10: K2tog, purl to last 2 sts, k2tog tbl (6 sts).

Bind off knitwise.

SEWING THE BEE

Weave in any loose ends to WS on all pieces, then block and steam both pairs of wings. With RS out, fold the body lengthwise and sew most of the seam using yarn A, leaving the top unsewn. Stuff the body with a small amount of yarn A, then finish sewing the seam. Sew the wings to the body using yarn C.

 SEE STEPS 10–12

FINISHING

Weave in any loose ends to WS on all pieces. Fold upper piece lengthwise RS together and sew the seam using yarn A, beginning at the cast-on edge and ending at the marker (remove markers). Turn the upper piece RS out. Position the sole so that its cast-on edge is at center back of the upper section and the top seam of the upper piece is in the center of the bind-off edge of the sole. Sew in place on RS using blanket stitch and matching colored yarn. To prevent the bugs from getting lost in the wash, thread a piece of scrap cotton yarn through the corners of all the pieces and tie together loosely. Felt the bugs and boots together and allow to dry thoroughly, stuffing the boots with paper to enhance their shape if necessary. Using yarns B and C, embroider chain stitch onto the wings of each butterfly.

 SEE STEPS 13–15

Sew the bugs in place on the outer side of each boot.

10 Sew most of the seam of the bee's body, then roll up some yarn A and stuff it through the opening. Finish sewing the seam to complete the bee's body.

11 Position the first wing at one side of the body and sew securely in place using yarn C.

12 Sew the second wing to the other side of the body, making sure it is positioned symmetrically with the first wing.

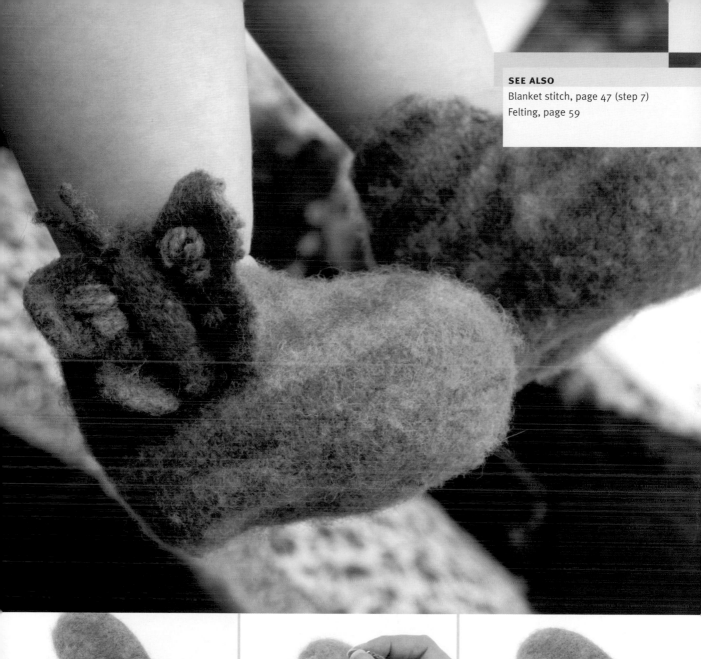

SEE ALSO
Blanket stitch, page 47 (step 7)
Felting, page 59

13 To work a chain stitch, bring the yarn needle to the front, then take it to the back at the same place. Bring it to the front again farther along, up through the loop of yarn.

14 Take the needle over the loop of yarn and through to the back again to secure the end of the chain stitch in place.

15 Decorate each wing with two chain stitches in yarn B at the top and one chain stitch in yarn C at the bottom. Vary their lengths to echo the shape of the wings.

PROJECT 5

Felted Sunday boots

Sized for Mom, Dad, and the kids, these boots will keep the whole family warm. Knitted in a tweed-effect wool yarn on two needles, the Fair Isle effect is created by slipping stitches and is continued across the sole. After knitting, the socks are felted to create a beautiful blurring of the colors and then finished with zippers.

UPPER (MAKE 2)

Using size 9 (5.5 mm) needles and yarn A, cast on 81 [93, 117, 129] sts.

Row 1 (RS): Knit.

Row 2: Purl. Break off yarn A and join yarn B.

Row 3: Knit.

Row 4: Purl. Break off yarn B and join yarn E.

Row 5: K2, (sl 1, k3) to last 3 sts, sl 1, k2.

Row 6: P2, (sl 1, p3) to last 3 sts, sl 1, p2.

👁 SEE STEPS 1–2

Rows 7–8: Repeat rows 5–6 once. Break off yarn E and join yarn C.

Row 9: Knit.

Row 10: Purl.

Rows 11–12: Repeat rows 9–10 once. Break off yarn C and join yarn D.

Start shaping XS only as follows.

Row 13: (K1, k2tog) twice, k2, (sl 1, k3) to last 9 sts, sl 1, k2, (k2tog, k1) twice (77 sts).

Row 14: P6, (sl 1, p3) to last 7 sts, sl 1, p6.

Row 15: (K1, k2tog) twice, (sl 1, k3) to last 7 sts, sl 1, (k2tog, k1) twice (73 sts).

Row 16: P4, (sl 1, p3) to last 5 sts, sl 1, p4.

Continue S, M, and L only as follows.

Row 13: (Sl 1, k3) to last st, sl 1.

Row 14: (Sl 1, p3) to last st, sl 1.

Rows 15–16: Repeat rows 13–14 once.

1 Start the slip stitch pattern on row 5 by slipping the specified stitches from the left to the right needle without working them.

2 Continue the slip-stitch pattern on row 6 by slipping the same stitches from the left to the right needle without working them. This creates a Fair Isle effect.

BEFORE YOU START

MEASUREMENTS

XS [S, M, L]

XS—Extra small to fit 6-in. (15-cm) long foot

S—Small to fit 7-in. (18-cm) long foot

M—Medium to fit 9½-in. (24-cm) long foot

L—Large to fit 10¼-in. (26-cm) long foot

YARN

DK-weight tweed-effect yarn (100% pure new wool; approx. 123 yds/113 m per 2 oz/50 g ball) in 4 colors:

A Brown x 1 ball

B Green x 1 ball

C Red x 1 ball

D Mustard x 1 ball

Sport-weight tweed-effect yarn (100% pure new wool; approx. 120 yds/110 m per 1 oz/25 g ball) in 1 color:

E Rust x 1 [1, 2, 3] balls

Yarn E is used doubled throughout

OTHER MATERIALS

Two medium-weight closed-end zippers in matching colors; 6 in. (15 cm) long for XS and S sizes, and 7 in. (18 cm) long for M and L sizes

NEEDLES

Size 9 (5.5 mm)

GAUGE

23 sts x 36 rows = 4 in. (10 cm) in slip-stitch stripe pattern using size 9 (5.5 mm) needles after felting (see page 59)

ABBREVIATIONS

k—knit; **m1k**—make 1 stitch knitwise; **m1p**—make 1 stitch purlwise; **p**—purl; **RS**—right side; **sl**—slip stitch purlwise from left to right needle without working it, keeping yarn on WS of work; **st(s)**—stitch(es); **tog**—together; **WS**—wrong side

Continue pattern for all sizes as follows, alternating colors as set by rows 1–16 and shaping as instructed.

👁 **SEE STEPS 3–5**

Row 17: (K1, k2tog) twice, knit to last 6 sts, (k2tog, k1) twice (69 [89, 113, 125] sts).

Row 18: Purl.

Row 19 (XS only): Bind off 6 sts knitwise at beginning of row, then knit to end (63 sts).

Row 19 (S, M, and L only): As row 17 (85 [109, 121] sts).

Row 20 (XS only): Bind off 6 sts purlwise at beginning of row, then purl to end (57 sts).

Row 20 (S, M, and L only): Purl.

Row 21 (All sizes): (K1, k2tog) twice, (sl 1, k3) to last 7 sts, sl 1, (k2tog, k1) twice (53 [81, 105, 117] sts).

Row 22: P4, (sl 1, p3) to last 5 sts, sl 1, p4.

Row 23: (K1, k2tog) twice, k2, (sl 1, k3) to last 9 sts, sl 1, k2, (k2tog, k1) twice (49 [77, 101, 113] sts).

Row 24: P6, (sl 1, p3) to last 7 sts, sl 1, p6.

Row 25 (XS and L only): (K1, k2tog) twice, knit to last 6 sts, (k2tog, k1) twice (45 [109] sts).

Row 25 (S and M only): Bind off 8 sts knitwise at beginning of row, then knit to end (69 [93] sts).

Row 26 (XS and L only): Purl.

Row 26 (S and M only): Bind off 8 sts purlwise at beginning of row, then purl to end (61 [85] sts).

Row 27 (All sizes): (K1, k2tog) twice, knit to last 6 sts, (k2tog, k1) twice (41 [57, 81, 105] sts).

Row 28: Purl.

Row 29 (XS, S, and M only): (K1, k2tog) twice, k2, (sl 1, k3) to last 9 sts, sl 1, k2, (k2tog, k1) twice (37 [53, 77] sts).

Row 29 (L only): Bind off 12 sts knitwise at beginning of row, (sl 1, k3) to last st, sl 1 (93 sts).

Row 30 (XS, S, and M only): P2, (sl 1, p3) to last 3 sts, sl 1, p2.

Row 30 (L only): Bind off 12 sts purlwise at beginning of row, (sl 1, p3) to last st, sl 1 (81 sts).

Complete XS only as follows.

Row 31: K2, (sl 1, k3) to last 3 sts, sl 1, k2.

Row 32: P2, (sl 1, p3) to last 3 sts, sl 1, p2.

Rows 33–36: Beginning with a knit row, work four rows in stockinette stitch.

Row 37: (Sl 1, k3) to last st, sl 1.

Row 38: (Sl 1, p3) to last st, sl 1.

Bind off knitwise.

S, M, and L continue as follows.

Row 31: (K1, k2tog) twice, k2, (sl 1, k3) to last 9 sts, sl 1, k2, (k2tog, k1) twice (49 [73, 79] sts).

Row 32: P6, (sl 1, p3) to last 7 sts, sl 1, p6.

Row 33: (K1, k2tog) twice, knit to last 6 sts, (k2tog, k1) twice (45 [69, 73] sts).

Row 34: Purl.

Complete S only as follows.

Row 35: K1, k2tog, knit to last 3 sts, k2tog, k1 (43 sts).

Row 36: Purl.

Row 37: K1, (sl 1, k3) to last 2 sts, sl 1, k1.

Row 38: P1, (sl 1, p3) to last 2 sts, sl 1, p1.

Rows 39–40: Repeat rows 37–38 once.

Rows 41–44: Beginning with a knit row, work four rows in stockinette stitch.

3 The upper piece is shaped in several ways, including knitting two stitches together (k2tog) to decrease by one stitch.

4 Another shaping technique is to bind off stitches knitwise at the beginning of a RS row.

5 To keep the shaping symmetrical, the same number of stitches are bound off purlwise at the beginning of the following WS row.

Bind off knitwise.

M and L continue as follows.

Row 35: As row 33 (65 [69] sts).

Row 36: Purl.

Row 37: (K1, k2tog) twice, k2, (sl 1, k3) to last 9 sts, sl 1, k2, (k2tog, k1) twice (61 [65] sts).

Row 38: P6, (sl 1, p3) to last 7 sts, sl 1, p6.

Row 39: (K1, k2tog) twice, (sl 1, k3) to last 7 sts, sl 1, (k2tog, k1) twice (57 [61] sts).

Row 40: P4, (sl 1, p3) to last 5 sts, sl 1, p4.

Row 41: (K1, k2tog) twice, knit to last 6 sts, (k2tog, k1) twice (53 [57] sts).

Row 42: Purl.

Work another 20 [28] rows in pattern without shaping.
Bind off knitwise.

SOLE (MAKE 2)

Using size 9 (5.5 mm) needles and yarn A, cast on
5 [7, 5, 9] sts.

Row 1 (RS): Knit.

Row 2: P1, m1p, purl to last st, m1p, p1 (7 [9, 7, 11] sts).
Break off yarn A and join yarn B.

Row 3: K1, m1k, knit to last st, m1k, k1 (9 [11, 9, 13] sts).

Row 4: Purl. Break off yarn B and join yarn E.

Row 5 (XS and S only): K2 [3], sl 1, k3, sl 1, k2 [3].

Row 5 (M and L only): K1, m1k, k1, (sl 1, k3) once [twice], sl 1, k1, m1k, k1 (11 [15] sts).

Row 6 (All sizes): P2 [3, 3, 3], (sl 1, p3) to last 3 [4, 4, 4] sts, sl 1, p2 [3, 3, 3].

Rows 5–6 set the slip-stitch pattern as on the upper pieces.
Continue in pattern as set; the following instructions specify shapings and first row of slip-stitch band only.

Row 7: Pattern; m1k at each end for S only (9 [13, 11, 15] sts).

Row 8: Pattern.

Break off yarn E and join yarn C.

Row 9: Knit; m1k at each end for XS, M, and L only (11 [13, 13, 17] sts)

Row 10: Purl.

Row 11: Knit; m1k at each end for S only (11 [15, 13, 17] sts).

Row 12: Purl. Break off yarn C and join yarn D.

Row 13: K1 [3, 2, 2], (sl 1, k3) to last 2 [4, 3, 3] sts, sl 1, k1 [3, 2, 2].

Rows 14–16: Pattern; m1k at each end of row 15 for XS and S only (13 [17, 13, 17] sts).

Continue pattern, alternating colors as set by rows 1–16.

Rows 17–20: Beginning with a knit row, work four rows in stockinette stitch; m1k at each end of row 17 for M and L only; m1p at each end of row 20 for XS and S only
(15 [19, 15, 19] sts).

FELTING

This is a process of shrinking a woolen fabric by washing it in soapy water to bind the fibers together to create a more solid and fluffy fabric. Felting will not work with superwash wools, cottons, or synthetic yarns. It can be done by hand but is easier in a washing machine.

Felting is very much a case of trial and error, because the water temperature and agitation strength of each washing machine varies. Too cool a wash for too short a time and the fabric will not shrink enough; too hot a wash for too long and your knitting could resemble concrete. It is therefore a good idea to felt the gauge test swatch first, remembering to work a couple of extra stitches and rows to allow for the fabric edges rolling and to make measuring more accurate.

Wash the piece at 100°F (40°C) on your machine's quick or half-wash program (approx. 30–40 minute long) using about ½ cup of a detergent suitable for wool use. Putting a towel into the wash will contribute to the felting process. When the wash cycle is complete, ease the damp swatch into shape by patting and smoothing as necessary. Allow to air dry and then measure the swatch.

If the swatch is smaller than the specified gauge in the pattern, the piece has felted too much, so shorten the wash cycle. If it is larger, wash for a bit longer. It is important that you keep notes of all details while you experiment so that you can repeat it successfully with the finished project.

Row 21: K1 [3, 1, 1], (sl 1, k3) to last 2 [4, 2, 2] sts, sl 1, k1 [3, 1, 1].

Rows 22–24: Pattern.

Rows 25–28: Beginning with a knit row, work four rows in stockinette stitch; m1k at each end of row 25 for M and L only; m1p at each end of row 28 for XS and S only (17 [21, 17, 21] sts).

Row 29: K4 [3, 4, 4], (sl 1, k3) to last 5 [4, 5, 5] sts, sl 1, k4 [3, 4, 4].

Rows 30–32: Pattern.

Rows 33–36: Beginning with a knit row, work four rows in stockinette stitch; m1k at each end of row 33 for M and L only (17 [21, 19, 23] sts).

Row 37: K2 [0, 3, 3], (sl 1, k3) to last 3 [1, 4, 4] sts, sl 1, k2 [0, 3, 3].

Rows 38–40: Pattern.

Rows 41–44: Beginning with a knit row, work four rows in stockinette stitch; m1k at each end of row 43 for M and L only; p2tog at each end of row 44 for XS only (15 [21, 21, 25] sts).

Row 45: K3 [2, 2, 2], (sl 1, k3) to last 4 [3, 3, 3] sts, sl 1, k3 [2, 2, 2].

Rows 46–48: Pattern.

Rows 49–52: Beginning with a knit row, work four rows in stockinette stitch; m1k at each end of row 51 for M only; k2tog at each end of row 51 for XS only; p2tog at each end of row 52 for S only (13 [19, 23, 25] sts).

Complete XS only as follows.

Row 53: K2tog, k2, sl 1, k3, sl 1, k2, k2tog (11 sts).

Row 54: P2tog, p1, sl 1, p3, sl 1, p1, p2tog (9 sts).

Row 55: K2tog, sl 1, k3, sl 1, k2tog (7 sts).

Row 56: P2tog, p3, p2tog (5 sts).

Bind off knitwise.

Continue S, M, and L as follows.

Row 53: K3 [1, 4], (sl 1, k3) to last 4 [2, 5] sts, sl 1, k3 [1, 4].

Rows 54–56: Pattern.

Rows 57–60: Beginning with a knit row, work four rows in stockinette stitch; p2tog at each end of rows 58 and 60 for S only (15 [23, 25] sts).

Complete S only as follows.

Row 61: (K3, sl 1) three times, k3.

Row 62: P2tog, p1, (sl 1, p3) twice, sl 1, p1, p2tog (13 sts).

Row 63: K2tog, (sl 1, k3) twice, k2tog (11 sts).

Row 64: P2tog, p3, sl 1, p3, p2tog (9 sts).

Bind off knitwise.

Continue M and L as follows.

Row 61: K3 [2], (sl 1, k3) to last 4 [3] sts, sl 1, k3 [2].

Rows 62–64: Pattern.

Rows 65–68: Beginning with a knit row, work four rows in stockinette stitch.

Row 69: K1 [4], (sl 1, k3) to last 2 [5] sts, sl 1, k1 [4].

Rows 70–72: Pattern.

Row 73 (M only): K2tog, knit to last 2 sts, k2tog (21 sts).

Row 73 (L only): Knit (25 sts).

Rows 74–76 (Both sizes): Beginning with a purl row, work three rows in stockinette stitch.

Row 77: K2tog, (sl 1, k3) to last 3 sts, sl 1, k2tog (19 [23] sts).

Rows 78–80: Pattern; p2tog at each end of row 79 for M only (17 [23] sts).

Rows 81–84: Beginning with a knit row, work four rows in

6 Fold the upper piece RS together and sew the center front seam using a fine backstitch.

7 With RS facing you, pin the zipper in place so that the edges of the fabric reach the zipper teeth. Using sewing thread in a toning color, sew the edge of the zipper in place on the WS.

8 Bring the needle to the front of the work and sew it in place along the edge of the fabric using backstitch. Remove the pins when you have finished.

SEE ALSO
Blanket stitch, page 47 (step 7)
Felting, page 59

stockinette stitch; k2tog at each end of rows 81 and 83 for
M only; k2tog at each end of row 83 for L only (13 [21] sts).

Row 85: K2tog, k1 [0], (sl 1, k3) once [four] times, sl 1, k1 [0],
k2tog (9 [19] sts).

Row 86 (M only): P2tog, pattern to last 2 sts, p2tog (7 sts).
Bind off knitwise.

Complete L as follows.

Row 86: Pattern (19 sts).

Row 87: K2tog, k3, (sl 1, k3) three times, k2tog (17 sts).

Row 88: P4, (sl 1, p3) to last st, p1.

Rows 89–94: Beginning with a knit row, work six rows
in stockinette stitch; k2tog at each end of rows 89, 91,
and 93; p2tog at each end of rows 92 and 94 (7 sts).
Bind off knitwise.

FINISHING

Weave in any loose ends to WS on all pieces. Fold the upper
pieces lengthwise with RS facing. Sew the center front seam,
beginning at cast-on edge and finishing at start of
decreasing.

 SEE STEP 6

Turn the upper piece RS out. Position the sole so that its cast-on
edge is at the center back of the upper section and the top seam
of the upper piece is in the center of the bind-off edge of the sole.
Sew in place on RS using blanket stitch and matching colored
yarn. Repeat for the other boot. Felt the boots and allow to dry
thoroughly, stuffing them with paper to enhance the shape if
necessary. When dry, sew a zipper in place.

 SEE STEPS 7–8

PROJECT 6

Side-seam socks

This project gives a twist to the conventional sock shape by working the sole and upper as separate pieces like boots, and placing the upper seam at the side of the foot. The print-effect yarn used for the upper piece contrasts with the plain colored sole.

LEFT UPPER

Using size 5 (3.75 mm) needles and yarn A, cast on 50 sts. Starting at the bottom right of the chart on page 66 and beginning with a knit row, work rows 1–40 in stockinette stitch and shape the sides as indicated. Increase on RS rows by k1f&b; increase on WS rows by p1f&b. Decrease at the beginning of a row by k2tog tbl on RS rows and p2tog tbl on WS rows. Decrease at the end of a row by k2tog on RS rows and p2tog on WS rows.

1 Increase by one stitch on RS rows using k1f&b. Simply knit into the front of the next stitch, then knit into the back of the same stitch.

BEFORE YOU START

MEASUREMENTS
Length from heel to toe (adjustable):
9½ in. (24 cm)
Length from top to heel (adjustable):
5½ in. (14 cm)

YARN
DK-weight yarn (100% merino wool;
approx. 176 yds/160 m per 2 oz/50 g
ball) x 2 colors:
A Variegated x 2 balls
B Blue x 1 ball

NEEDLES
Size 5 (3.75 mm)

GAUGE
24 sts x 34 rows = 4 in. (10 cm)
in stockinette stitch using size 5
(3.75 mm) needles

ABBREVIATIONS
k—knit; **k1f&b**—knit into front
and back of same stitch; **p** –purl;
p1f&b –purl into front and back
of same stitch; **RS**—right side;
sl—slip stitch from left to right needle
without working it; **st(s)**—stitch(es);
tbl—through back of loop;
tog—together; **WS**—wrong side

 SEE STEPS 1–6
BELOW AND OVERLEAF

Work right-hand side of chart for rows 41–46. When the right-hand side has been shaped, rejoin the yarn on row 41 where indicated with * on the chart.

 SEE STEPS 7–8 OVERLEAF

Bind off 7 sts knitwise and complete the other side of the upper. End after row 92, with RS facing for next row (19 sts). Shape the toe as follows.
Row 93: K1, k2tog tbl, knit to last 3 sts, k2tog, k1 (17 sts).
Row 94: (P1, p2tog) twice, p3, (p2tog tbl, p1) twice (13 sts).
Row 95: *K1, (k2tog tbl) twice; repeat from * to last st, k1 (9 sts).
Bind off purlwise.

RIGHT UPPER

Using size 5 (3.75 mm) needles and yarn A, cast on 50 sts. Work as for the left upper but begin with a purl row. On row 41, when the right-hand side has been shaped, rejoin the yarn where

indicated with * on the chart to complete the other side of the upper. End after row 92, with RS facing for next row. Shape the toe as follows.
Row 93: P1, p2tog, purl to last 3 sts, p2tog tbl, p1 (17 sts).
Row 94: (K1, k2tog tbl) twice, k3, (k2tog, k1) twice (13 sts).
Row 95: *P1, (p2tog) twice; repeat from * to last st, p1.
Bind off knitwise.

SOLE (MAKE 2)

Using size 5 (3.75 mm) needles and yarn B, cast on 6 sts. Starting at the bottom right of the chart on page 67 and beginning with a knit row, work in stockinette stitch, shaping the sides (using same techniques as left upper) and placing slip stitches as indicated.

 SEE STEP 9 OVERLEAF

Begin with a knit row when working the left sole; begin with a purl row when working the right sole. When the final row of the chart has been completed, bind off purlwise.

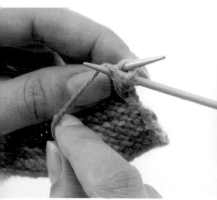

2 Increase by one stitch on WS rows using p1f&b. Simply purl into the front of the next stitch, then purl into the back of the same stitch.

3 Use k2tog tbl to decrease by one stitch at the beginning of a RS row. Insert the right needle knitwise through the back of the loops of the next two stitches and work together.

4 Use p2tog tbl to decrease by one stitch at the beginning of a WS row. Insert the right needle purlwise through the back of the loops of the next two stitches and work together.

KEY

	Yarn **A**
	Yarn **B**
*	Rejoin yarn here
▽	Sl 1

5 Decrease by one stitch at the end of RS rows using k2tog. Insert the right needle knitwise through the front of the loops of the next two stitches and work together.

6 Decrease by one stitch at the end of WS rows using p2tog. Insert the right needle purlwise through the front of the loops of the next two stitches and work together.

7 When you are ready to work the left-hand side of the upper piece, use the right needle to pick up an extra loop of yarn just to the right of the first stitch.

The chart shows row numbers on the right side (odd numbers): 85, 83, 81, 79, 77, 75, 73, 71, 69, 67, 65, 63, 61, 59, 57, 55, 53, 51, 49, 47, 45, 43, 41, 39, 37, 35, 33, 31, 29, 27, 25, 23, 21, 19, 17, 15, 13, 11, 9, 7, 5, 3, 1

ADJUSTING THE SIZE

You can increase the length of the foot to give a better fit for a man by adjusting the number of rows of stockinette stitch worked between rows 38 and 39 on the sole, and rows 53 and 54 on the upper. Alter the length of the leg section on the upper by working extra rows of stockinette stitch before starting to work from the chart.

FINISHING

Weave in any loose ends to WS on all pieces, then block and steam gently. Fold the upper piece in half lengthwise so that RS are together and side edges align. Sew the side seam using yarn A. With RS of upper and sole pieces together, position the sole so that cast-on and bind-off stitches are centered at toe and heel and sew the sole in place using yarn B.

👁 SEE STEP 10

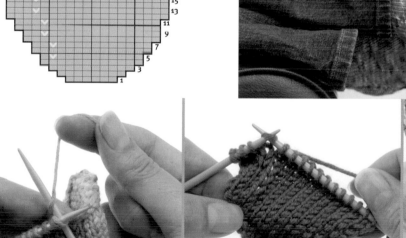

8 Transfer this loop to the left needle, then rejoin the yarn and work the loop and first stitch together. This will help to eliminate any gaping at the join.

9 The sole has a slip-stitch detail running along one side. Where indicated on the chart, slip the next stitch from the left to the right needle without working it.

10 Position the sole and upper RS together, making sure that the toe and heel of the sole are centered in the upper. Sew together using a fine backstitch.

PROJECT 7

Beaded Argyle socks

These socks are knitted on two needles using a beautifully soft merino wool yarn. A luxurious wool/cashmere blend yarn can be substituted if you are feeling more extravagant. The classic Argyle pattern is created using a combination of beads and Swiss-darned embroidery.

KNITTING THE SOCKS (MAKE 2)

Thread 42 beads onto yarn A. Using size 2 (2.75 mm) needles and yarn A, cast on 58 sts and then change to yarn B. Starting at the bottom right of the chart on page 71, work 12 rows in k1, p1 rib, using the colors indicated on the chart and carrying the yarns up the side of the work. Change to size 3 (3.25 mm) needles and continue in stockinette stitch, starting with a knit row. The chart represents one side of the sock. The Argyle design and shaping are symmetrical on each side, so work from right to left across each row, then work back from left to right across the same row. Move up to the next row and repeat this process. Decrease at the beginning of a row by k2tog tbl; decrease at the end of a row by k2tog. Note that the beads are knitted into the socks at this stage, but the Swiss darning is added after the knitting is finished. After working row 62 of the chart, follow the written instructions to complete the sock.

👁 **SEE STEPS 1–3**

HEEL—FIRST SIDE

Row 1 (RS): K15 and turn.
Row 2 & all unspecified WS rows: Purl.
Row 3: K14 and turn.
Row 5: K13 and turn.
Row 7: K12 and turn.
Row 9: K11 and turn.
Row 11: K10 and turn.
Row 13: K9 and turn.
Row 15: K8 and turn.
Row 17: K7 and turn.
Row 18: Purl all 7 sts.
Row 19: K8 and turn.
Row 21: K9 and turn.
Row 23: K10 and turn.
Row 25: K11 and turn.
Row 27: K12 and turn.
Row 29: K13 and turn.
Row 31: K14 and turn.
Row 33: K15 and turn.
Row 35: Knit across all 54 sts.

HEEL—SECOND SIDE

Row 1 (WS): P15 and turn.
Row 2 & all unspecified RS rows: Knit.
Row 3: P14 and turn.
Row 5: P13 and turn.
Row 7: P12 and turn.

BEFORE YOU START

MEASUREMENTS

Length from heel to toe: 9 in. (23 cm)
Length from top to heel: 8 in. (20 cm)

YARN

Sport-weight yarn (100% merino wool; approx. 191 yds/175 m per 2 oz/50 g ball) in 3 colors:

A Beige x 2 balls
B Cream x small amount for rib and embroidery
C Blue x small amount for rib and embroidery

OTHER MATERIALS

84 small green beads

NEEDLES

Size 2 (2.75 mm)
Size 3 (3.25 mm)

GAUGE

28 sts x 38 rows = 4 in. (10 cm) in stockinette stitch using size 3 (3.25 mm) needles

ABBREVIATIONS

bead 1—place 1 bead; **k**—knit; **p**—purl; **RS**—right side; **st(s)**—stitch(es); **tbl**—through back of loop; **tog**—together; **WS**—wrong side

1 To place a bead, bring the yarn to the front of the work and slide the bead up the yarn until it sits in front of the right needle.

2 Slip the next stitch purlwise from the left to right needle without working it.

3 Take the yarn to the back of the work and knit the next stitch, making sure that the bead sits in front of the slipped stitch on the RS of the work.

Row 9: P11 and turn.
Row 11: P10 and turn.
Row 13: P9 and turn.
Row 15: P8 and turn.
Row 17: P7 and turn.
Row 18: Knit all 7 sts.
Row 19: P8 and turn.
Row 21: P9 and turn.
Row 23: P10 and turn.
Row 25: P11 and turn.
Row 27: P12 and turn.
Row 29: P13 and turn.
Row 31: P14 and turn.
Row 33: P15 and turn.
Row 35: Purl across all 54 sts, ending with RS facing.

FOOT AND TOE

Rows 1–52: Beginning with a knit row, work 52 rows in stockinette stitch, ending with RS facing for toe shaping.
Row 53 (RS): K11, k2tog, k2, k2tog tbl, k20, k2tog, k2, k2tog tbl, k11 (50 sts).
Row 54 & all WS rows: Purl.
Row 55: K10, k2tog, k2, k2tog tbl, k18, k2tog, k2, k2tog tbl, k10 (46 sts).
Row 57: K9, k2tog, k2, k2tog tbl, k16, k2tog, k2, k2tog tbl, k9 (42 sts).
Row 59: K8, k2tog, k2, k2tog tbl, k14, k2tog, k2, k2tog tbl, k8 (38 sts).

ADJUSTING THE SIZE

To make the socks a little larger to give a more comfortable fit for a man, measure around the ankle, just above the joint, and multiply this figure by 7 if you are working in imperial or 2.8 if you are working in metric—this is the number of sts you will need per 1 in. (1 cm). For example, if the ankle measures 9 in. (23 cm): 9 x 7 = 63 sts; 23 x 2.8 = 64 sts. Round up or down to the nearest even number, then add 4 sts to account for the leg shaping. Cast on this number of stitches and work more rows of stockinette stitch in the leg section if required; work more rows in the foot section as well (between rows 1 and 52). Take care that you keep the shaping correct, and adjust the position of the Argyle pattern if necessary. This type of adjustment is not suitable for beginners. For a more traditional look, omit the beads and add the cross design using Swiss darning.

4 To work Swiss darning, thread a yarn needle with the required color. Bring the needle through to the front of the work at the base of the first stitch to be covered.

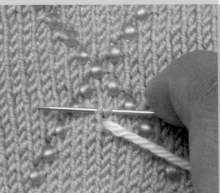

5 Pass the needle underneath both loops of the stitch above.

6 Take the needle from front to back through the base of the original stitch (where it first came out), covering one stitch.

Row 61: K7, k2tog, k2, k2tog tbl, k12, k2tog, k2, k2tog tbl, k7 (34 sts).
Row 63: K6, k2tog, k2, k2tog tbl, k10, k2tog, k2, k2tog tbl, k6 (30 sts).
Row 65: K5, k2tog, k2, k2tog tbl, k8, k2tog, k2, k2tog tbl, k5 (26 sts).
Row 67: K4, k2tog, k2, k2tog tbl, k6, k2tog, k2, k2tog tbl, k4 (22 sts).
Row 69: K3, k2tog, k2, k2tog tbl, k4, k2tog, k2, k2tog tbl, k3 (18 sts).
Row 70: Purl.
Bind off knitwise.

FINISHING

Using yarns B and C and referring to the chart, embroider the motif using Swiss darning.

👁 **SEE STEPS 4–7**

Weave in any loose ends to WS on all the pieces, then block and steam gently. Fold the sock lengthwise, RS together, and sew the back seam using a fine backstitch. Turn RS out and fold so that the seam is at center back. Overcast the toe seam on the RS.

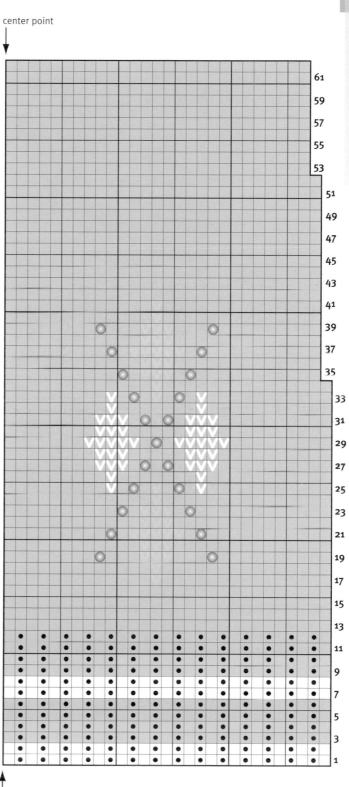

7 Bring the yarn through the base of the next stitch to be covered. Continue placing Swiss darning as indicated on the chart.

KEY

▢	Yarn **A**
▢	Yarn **B**
▢	Yarn **C**
▢	K on RS, p on WS
▣	P on RS, k on WS
◯	Bead 1
☑	Swiss darn

 **PROJECT 8**

Basic tubular socks

This basic sock pattern for adults is perfect for learning how to knit in the round. Worked in a self-patterning sock yarn on double-pointed needles, it allows you to get to grips with the basics of tubular sock knitting while the yarn creates beautiful jewel-like effects with no effort on your part.

GETTING THE SIZE RIGHT

This is a "Sunday slouching" type of sock, so the fit is quite generous. If you want a tighter fit, go for a smaller size. To ensure that your sock fits, measure around the ankle, just above the joint, and multiply this figure by 8.4 if you are working in imperial or 3.3 if you are working in metric—this is the number of sts you will need per 1 in. (1 cm). For example, if your ankle measures 9 in. (23 cm): 9 x 8.4 = 75.6 sts; 23 x 3.3 sts = 75.9 sts. Round down to 74 sts and follow the instructions for the medium size.

BEFORE YOU START

MEASUREMENTS

Small [medium, large]
Ankle circumference: 8¼ [9, 9½] in.
(21 [23, 24.5] cm)
Leg length and foot length are adjustable

YARN

Sport-weight self-patterning sock yarn
(45% cotton, 42% pure new wool,
13% polyamide; approx. 415 yds/380 m
per 4 oz/100 g ball) x 1 ball for short
socks or 2 balls for long socks (variegated
orange/pink)

NEEDLES

Five size 2 (2.5 mm) double-pointed
needles

GAUGE

33 sts x 40 rows = 4 in. (10 cm)
in stockinette stitch using size 2
(2.5 mm) needles

ABBREVIATIONS

dpn(s)—double-pointed needle(s);
k—knit; **k1f&b**—knit into front and back
of same stitch; **p**—purl; **RS**—right side;
skpo—slip 1 stitch, knit 1 stitch, pass
slip stitch over; **st(s)**—stitch(es);
tbl—through back of loop;
tog—together; **WS**—wrong side

KNITTING THE SOCKS (MAKE 2)

Using size 2 (2.5 mm) needles, cast on 68 [74, 80] sts and
divide as equally as possible onto three dpns. Take care not
to cast on too tightly. Place a marker after the last stitch to
mark the beginning of the round.
Round 1: (K1, p1) to end.

 SEE STEPS 1–2

Repeat round 1 until work measures 1½ in. (4 cm), ending
at marker and increasing by k1f&b at end of last round
(69 [75, 81] sts). Pull the yarn a little tighter than normal
when working the first stitch on each needle to avoid
creating any ladders between each set of stitches.
Continue working in rounds of stockinette stitch until leg
is the required length from end of rib—4 in. (10 cm) for a
short sock and 7 in. (18 cm) for a long sock.

HEEL FLAP

Knit 19 sts; these will form the heel flap. The remaining
50 [56, 62] sts will form the instep; divide these evenly
onto the other two dpns.

 SEE STEP 3

Working backward and forward in rows on the heel sts only,
turn and work as follows.

1 Cast on the required number of
stitches, then divide them onto
three dpns as evenly as possible.

2 Place a marker after the last
stitch that you cast on to mark
the beginning of each round, then
work the first round in k1, p1 rib.

3 To start the heel flap, knit 19 sts onto
one dpn, then divide the remaining
stitches onto the other two dpns.

Row 1 (WS): Purl.

Row 2 (RS): (K1, k1 tbl) to last st, k1.

Repeat rows 1–2 until heel flap is as long as it is wide, ending with a purl row (about 23 rows).

 SEE STEP 4

TURNING THE HEEL

Row 1 (RS): K14, turn.

Row 2: P9, turn.

Row 3: K8, k2tog, k1, turn (18 sts).

Row 4: P9, p2tog, p1, turn (17 sts).

Row 5: K10, k2tog, k1, turn (16 sts).

Row 6: P11, p2tog, p1, turn (15 sts).

Row 7: K12, k2tog, turn (14 sts).

Row 8: P12, p2tog, turn (13 sts).

Row 9: Knit.

 SEE STEP 5

Pick up and knit 9 sts down left side of heel flap, place marker, then k10 [13, 16]. Using another dpn, knit the next 30 sts. Using another dpn, k10 [13, 16], place marker, then pick up and knit 9 sts down right side of heel flap. Using another dpn, k6 (81 [87, 93] sts), then transfer them onto the previous dpn. The beginning of round is now at center back.

 SEE STEPS 6–7

GUSSET

Round 1: K14, k2tog, slip marker, k50 [56, 62], slip marker, skpo, knit to end.

Round 2: Knit.

Round 3: Knit to within 2 sts of marker, k2tog, slip marker, knit to next marker, slip marker, skpo, knit to end.

Rounds 4–11: Repeat rounds 2–3 four times 69 [75, 81] sts. Work to end of round, then rearrange sts so they are evenly divided onto three dpns, keeping beginning of round at center back.

 SEE STEP 8

FOOT AND TOE

Knit in rounds until foot is 1½ in. (4 cm) shorter than desired finished length.

Rearrange sts on needles as follows, discarding the markers: 1st dpn—18 [20, 21] sts; 2nd dpn—34 [37, 40] sts; 3rd dpn—17 [18, 20] sts.

 SEE STEP 9

Remembering that rounds begin at center bottom of foot, shape the toe as follows.

Round 1: 1st dpn—k2tog, knit to last 3 sts, k2tog, k1; 2nd dpn—k1, k2tog tbl, knit to last 3 sts, k2tog, k1; 3rd dpn—k2tog tbl, knit to end.

Round 2: Knit.

Round 3: 1st dpn—knit to last 3 sts, k2tog, k1;

4 Work the heel flap back and forth in rows until it is as long as it is wide. The heel flap is worked in a special "heel stitch" (k1, k1 tbl on RS rows) to reinforce it.

5 Use short-row shaping to "turn the heel." This shapes the knitted piece without binding off stitches and is used to create a rounded base on the heel.

6 Before you can complete the foot, you need to prepare the stitches for working in rounds again. Start by picking up and knitting 9 sts down the left side of the heel flap; place a marker.

2nd dpn—k1, k2tog tbl, knit to last
3 sts, k2tog, k1; 3rd dpn—k2tog tbl,
knit to end.
Rounds 4–11: Repeat rounds 1–2
four times.
Round 12: Knit.
Rounds 13–15: Repeat round 3
three times.
Slip the sts from 1st dpn onto end
of 3rd dpn.

FINISHING

Weave in any loose ends to WS on
all pieces, then block and steam
gently. Graft the toe seam.

SEE ALSO
Circular knitting using dpns,
page 30
Grafting, page 24

7 Knit the stitches of the instep, place
a marker, then pick up and knit
9 sts up the right side of the heel
flap. Knit to the center of the heel;
this is the beginning of the round.

8 Work the gusset as instructed,
then rearrange the stitches evenly
onto three dpns, remembering
that rounds begin at center back.
Keep the markers in place.

9 After working the foot, rearrange
the stitches onto three dpns to start
shaping the toe.

 **PROJECT 9**

Spiral heelless socks

This project is knitted using the magic loop technique. Although this takes some practice to master, it is well worth persevering because it allows you to knit a narrow tube using a single circular needle. Here, it is combined with a rib structure that causes the fabric to spiral, so there is no need to work a heel. The sock is worked from the toe up to the top rib.

1 Cast on 20 sts, then pull the cord between the 11th and 12th stitches so that the stitches are divided roughly in half, ready to start working in rounds.

KNITTING THE SOCKS (MAKE 2)

Using a size 4 (3.5 mm) circular needle, cast on 20 sts and follow the pattern using the magic loop technique (page 31). In this case, start by pulling the cord between the 11th and 12th stitches.

 SEE STEP 1

Place a marker in front of the 1st stitch.
Round 1: Knit.

 SEE STEPS 2–3

Round 2: (K1, m1k, k8, m1k, k1) twice (24 sts).
Round 3: (K1, m1k, k10, m1k, k1) twice (28 sts).
Round 4: (K1, m1k, k12, m1k, k1) twice (32 sts).
Round 5: (K1, m1k, k14, m1k, k1) twice (36 sts).
Round 6: (K1, m1k, k16, m1k, k1) twice (40 sts).
Round 7: (K1, m1k, k18, m1k, k1) twice (44 sts).
Round 8: Knit.
Round 9: (K1, m1k, k20, m1k, k1) twice (48 sts).
Round 10: Knit.

Round 11: P1, m1k, (k2, p2) 5 times, k2, m1k, p1, k1, m1k, p2, (p2, k2) 5 times, m1k, k1 (52 sts).
Rounds 12–14: (P2, k2) to end.
*Round 15: K1, (p2, k2) to last 3 sts, p2, k1.
Rounds 16–18: As round 15.
Rounds 19–22: (K2, p2) to end.
Rounds 23–26: P1, (k2, p2) to last 3 sts, k2, p1.
Rounds 27–30: (P2, k2) to end.*

 **SEE STEP 4**

Repeat from * to * four times. The sock should measure 9 in. (23 cm) long. Change to a size 3 (3 mm) circular needle to work the top rib.
Work each round as (p2, k2) to last 2 sts, p2 until top rib measures 2 in. (5 cm) long. Bind off in rib, taking care not to do so too tightly.

FINISHING

Weave in any loose ends to WS on all pieces; do not block or steam. Turn RS out and overcast the toe seam.

BEFORE YOU START

MEASUREMENTS

Length from top to toe: 12¼ in. (31 cm)

YARN

DK-weight yarn (100% alpaca; approx. 131 yds/120 m per 2 oz/50 g ball) x 2 balls (variegated orange)

NEEDLES

32-in. (80-cm) long size 4 (3.5 mm) circular needle
32-in. (80-cm) long size 3 (3 mm) circular needle

GAUGE

23 sts x 32 rows = 4 in. (10 cm) in stockinette stitch using size 4 (3.5 mm) needle

ABBREVIATIONS

k—knit; **m1k**—make 1 stitch knitwise; **p**—purl; **RS**—right side; **st(s)**—stitch(es); **WS**—wrong side

2 Work the first half of round 1 until the left needle is empty. Pull the cord down through the stitches on the cord until they slide up onto the left needle.

3 Slide the stitches from the right needle down onto the cord so that the right needle is free to work the second half of round 1.

4 The p2, k2 rib structure is staggered from one round to the next to create a spiraling texture. Remember to keep count carefully to ensure the pattern stays correct up the whole sock.

 **PROJECT 10**

Pompom bobby socks

These funkily colored socks are worked in a stretchy self-patterning polyester,

polyamide, and wool blend yarn that is perfect for socks because it provides strength

and elasticity. The rolled edge is knitted in a single-color yarn for contrast, and the back

of the ankle is finished with a cute pompom. Worked on two needles with a top seam,

these socks are very easy to make.

KNITTING THE SOCKS (MAKE 2)

Using size 3 (3.25 mm) needles and yarn B, cast on 32 sts.

Rows 1–7: Beginning with a knit row, work 7 rows in stockinette stitch.

Row 8 (WS): P2tog, (p8, p2tog) to end (28 sts).

Row 9: Knit.

Break off yarn, leaving sts on needle. Using yarn B, cast 32 sts onto the empty needle. Repeat rows 1–9, ending with both pieces on the same needle after row 9. Do not break off the yarn.

Row 10: Purl across both sets of stitches (56 sts).

Row 11 (RS): Purl.

 SEE STEPS 1–3

Break off yarn B and join yarn A.

Rows 12–24: Beginning with a purl row, work 12 rows in stockinette stitch.

HEEL

Row 1 (RS): K43, wrap st, turn.
Row 2: P29, wrap st, turn.
Row 3: K28, wrap st, turn.
Row 4: P27, wrap st, turn.
Row 5: K26, wrap st, turn.
Row 6: P25, wrap st, turn.
Row 7: K24, wrap st, turn.

Row 8: P23, wrap st, turn.
Row 9: K22, wrap st, turn.
Row 10: P21, wrap st, turn.
Row 11: K20, wrap st, turn.
Row 12: P19, wrap st, turn.
Row 13: K18, wrap st, turn.
Row 14: P17, wrap st, turn.
Row 15: K16, wrap st, turn.
Row 16: P15, wrap st, turn.

On following rows, work each wrap bar and slip stitch together as one.

Row 17: K16 and turn.
Row 18: P17 and turn.
Row 19: K18 and turn.
Row 20: P19 and turn.
Row 21: K20 and turn.
Row 22: P21 and turn.
Row 23: K22 and turn.
Row 24: P23 and turn.
Row 25: K24 and turn.
Row 26: P25 and turn.
Row 27: K26 and turn.
Row 28: P27 and turn.
Row 29: K28 and turn.
Row 30: P29 and turn.
Row 31: K30 and turn.
Row 32: Purl all sts.

Rows 33–90: Beginning with a knit row, work 58 rows in stockinette stitch or until foot measures 6 in. (15 cm) from end of heel.

BEFORE YOU START

MEASUREMENTS

Length from heel to toe: 9¼ in. (23.5 cm)

YARN

A Sport-weight yarn (70% wool, 23% polyamide, 7% polyester; approx. 230 yds/210 m per 2 oz/50 g ball) x 2 balls (bright multicolors)
B Sport-weight yarn (100% merino wool; approx. 200 yds/183 m per 2 oz/50 g ball) x 1 ball (white)

NEEDLES

Size 3 (3.25 mm)

GAUGE

29 sts x 44 rows = 4 in. (10 cm) in stockinette stitch using size 3 (3.25 mm) needles

ABBREVIATIONS

k—knit; **p**—purl; **RS**—right side; **st(s)**—stitch(es); **tbl**—through back of loop; **tog**—together; **wrap st**—see pages 97–99 (steps 3–8); **WS**—wrong side

1 Work the first half of the rolled top of the sock, then break off the yarn without binding off the stitches. Cast 32 sts onto the empty needle.

2 Work the second half of the rolled top in the same way as the first half, keeping the first half on one of the needles throughout.

3 On row 10, purl across both sets of stitches to join them together. Repeat to complete the rolled top.

4 Fold the sock RS together and sew the top seam of the main section of the sock using yarn A and a fine backstitch.

5 Fold the sock WS together to sew the front seam of the rolled top. This is so that the stitching will be hidden when the top rolls outward.

6 Cut out two cardboard circles 1 in. (2.5 cm) larger than the pompom you are making. Cut a small wedge out of each circle, then cut out a central 1 in. (2.5 cm) hole.

SEE ALSO
Wrap stitch, pages 97–99
(steps 3–8)

TOE

Row 1 (RS): (K11, k2tog, k2, k2tog tbl, k11) twice (52 sts).

Row 2 & all WS rows: Purl.

Row 3: Knit.

Row 5: (K10, k2tog, k2, k2tog tbl, k10) twice (48 sts).

Row 7: Knit.

Row 9: (K9, k2tog, k2, k2tog tbl, k9) twice (44 sts).

Row 11: (K8, k2tog, k2, k2tog tbl, k8) twice (40 sts).

Row 13: (K7, k2tog, k2, k2tog tbl, k7) twice (36 sts).

Row 15: (K6, k2tog, k2, k2tog tbl, k6) twice (32 sts).

Row 16: (P5, p2tog tbl, p2, p2tog, p5) twice (28 sts).

Row 17: (K4, k2tog, k2, k2tog tbl, k4) twice (24 sts).

Row 18: Purl.

Bind off knitwise.

FINISHING

Weave in any loose ends to WS on all pieces, then block and steam gently. Fold the sock in half lengthwise, with RS together, and sew the colored section of the top seam using a fine backstitch and yarn A. Turn RS out and complete the top seam by sewing the rolled top using a fine backstitch and yarn B.

👁 SEE STEPS 4–5

Refold the sock so that seam is at center front. Overcast the toe seam on the RS. Using yarns A and B together, make a 1-in. (2.5-cm) diameter pompom for each sock.

👁 SEE STEPS 6–9

Sew each pompom in place at the back of the ankle.

7 Hold the circles together and wrap the yarn around the circles until they are completely covered. Do this using one end of yarn A and one end of yarn B together.

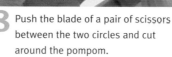

8 Push the blade of a pair of scissors between the two circles and cut around the pompom.

9 Tie a piece of yarn around the center of the pompom as tightly as possible. Remove the cardboard circles and trim the pompom to form a neat ball.

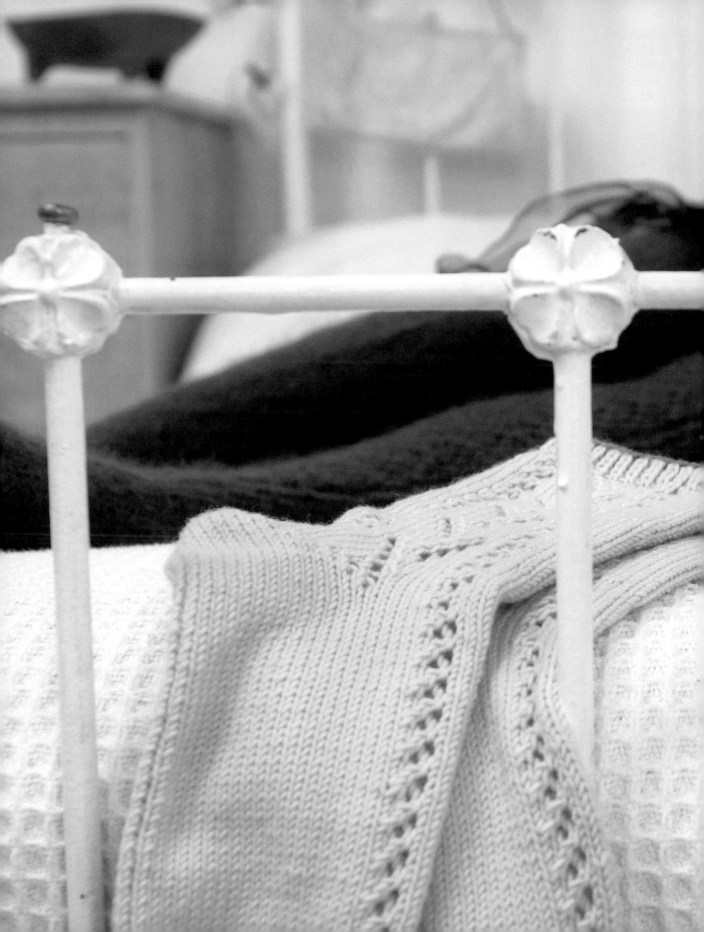

PROJECT 11

Love-heart slippers

These slippers, shaped liked ballet pumps, are worked in a soft pink yarn on two needles. The love-heart motif is created by knitting beads into the uppers, but would look just as effective worked in Swiss darning (see project 7). Sew suede patches onto the soles to prevent slipping if you wish.

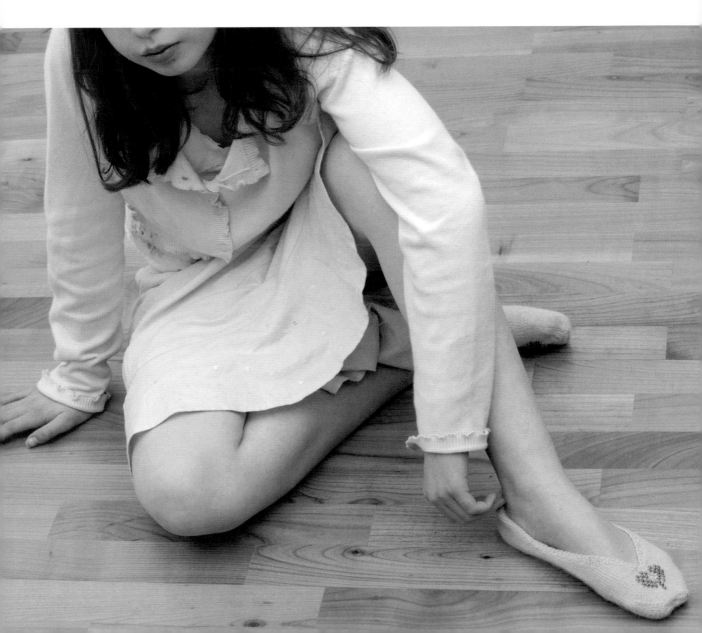

KNITTING THE SLIPPERS (MAKE 2)

Using size 1 (2.25 mm) needles, cast on 19 sts.

Row 1 (RS): Knit.

Row 2: K1, purl to last 2 sts, k2.

Row 3: Knit to last 2 sts, m1k, knit to end (20 sts).

Row 4: K1, purl to last 2 sts, k2.

Row 5–18: Repeat rows 3–4 seven times (27 sts).

Row 19: Knit.

Row 20: K1, purl to last 2 sts, k2.

Rows 21–28: Repeat rows 19–20 three times.

Row 29: K2, k2tog tbl, knit to end (26 sts).

Row 30: K1, purl to last 2 sts, k2.

Row 31: Knit.

Row 32: K1, purl to last 2 sts, k2.

Row 33: K2, k2tog tbl, knit to end (25 sts).

Rows 34–49: Repeat rows 30–33 four times, placing marker in last decrease (21 sts).

 See steps 1–2

Row 50: K1, purl to last 2 sts, k2.

Row 51: Knit.

Row 52: K1, purl to last 2 sts, k2.

Repeat rows 51–52 until work measures ⅜ [¾] in. (1 [2] cm) from marker, ending with RS facing for next row.

Begin increasing as follows.

Row 1: K2, m1k, knit to end (22 sts).

Row 2: K1, purl to last 2 sts, k2.

Row 3: Knit.

Row 4: K1, purl to last 2 sts, k2.

Rows 5–16: Repeat rows 1–4 three times (25 sts).

Row 17: K2, m1k, knit to end (26 sts).

Row 18: K1, purl to last 2 sts, k2.

Row 19: Knit

Row 20: K1, purl to last 2 sts, m1k, k2 (27 sts).

Row 21: Knit.

Row 22: K1, purl to last 2 sts, k2.

Rows 23–34: Repeat rows 18–22 twice (31 sts).

Row 35: K2, m1k, knit to end (32 sts).

Row 36: K1, purl to last 2 sts, k2.

Break off yarn and leave sts on needle, sliding them out of the way while you work the second side.

 See step 3

Before you start

MEASUREMENTS

1st size

To fit 8¼-in. (21-cm) long foot

2nd size

To fit 9-in. (23-cm) long foot

YARN

Sport-weight yarn (35% cotton, 25% polyamide, 18% angora, 13% viscose, 9% cashmere; approx. 197 yds/180 m per 2 oz/50 g ball) x 1 ball (pink)

OTHER MATERIALS

8 small clear beads

70 large pink beads

NEEDLES

Size 1 (2.25 mm)

GAUGE

33 sts x 48 rows = 4 in. (10 cm) in stockinette stitch using size 1 (2.25 mm) needles

ABBREVIATIONS

bead 1—place 1 bead; **k**—knit; **m1k**—make 1 stitch knitwise; **p**—purl; **RS**—right side; **st(s)**—stitch(es); **tbl**—through back of loop; **tog**—together; **WS**—wrong side

1 Fold a scrap of contrasting colored yarn in half and thread the center through a yarn needle. Insert the needle through the last decrease on row 49 and pull the loop through.

2 Remove the needle, then insert the ends of yarn through the loop and pull tight. Alternatively, use a ready-made plastic marker.

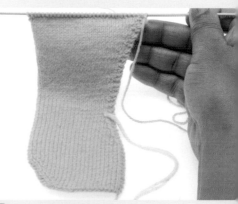

3 When you have finished shaping the first side, break off the yarn but do not bind off. Slide the stitches to the end of the needle.

SECOND SIDE
Thread beads onto the yarn as follows:
11 pink, 1 clear, 4 pink, 2 clear, 4 pink,
1 clear, 12 pink.

 SEE STEPS 4–5

Cast 19 sts onto the needle holding the
stitches from the first side.

 SEE STEP 6

Row 1 (RS): Knit.
Row 2: K2, purl to last st, k1.
Row 3: K2, m1k, knit to end (20 sts).
Row 4: K2, purl to last st, k1.
Rows 5–18: Repeat rows 3–4 seven times
(27 sts).
Row 19: Knit.
Row 20: K2, purl to last st, k1.
Rows 21–28: Repeat rows 19–20 three
times.
Row 29: Knit to last 4 sts, k2tog, k2
(26 sts).
Row 30: K2, purl to last st, k1.
Row 31: Knit.
Row 32: K2, purl to last st, k1.
Rows 33–48: Repeat rows 29–32 four
times.

Row 49: Repeat row 29, placing marker
in last decrease (21 sts).
Row 50: K2, purl to last st, k1.
Row 51: Knit.
Row 52: K2, purl to last st, k1.
Repeat rows 51–52 until work measures
³⁄₈ [³⁄₄] in. (1 [2] cm) from marker, with
RS facing for next row.
Begin increasing as follows.
Row 1: Knit to the last 2 sts, m1k, knit to
end (22 sts).
Row 2: K2, purl to last st, k1.
Row 3: Knit.
Row 4: K2, purl to last st, k1.
Rows 5–16: Repeat rows 1–4 three times
(25 sts).
Row 17: Knit to last 2 sts, m1k, knit to
end (26 sts).
Row 18: K2, purl to last st, k1.
Row 19: Knit.
Row 20: K2, m1k, purl to last st, k1
(27 sts).
Row 21: Knit.
Row 22: K2, purl to last st, k1.
Rows 23–34: Repeat rows 17–22 twice
(31 sts).
Row 35: Knit to last 2 sts, m1k, knit to
end (32 sts).
Row 36: K2, purl to last st, k1.

JOINING THE TWO SIDES
Knit to last 3 sts, k2tog tbl, k1.
Working straight across onto the stitches
from the first side of the foot (RS facing):
k1, k2tog, knit to end (62 sts).

 SEE STEP 7

Row 2: K1, p29, k2, p29, k1.
Row 3: Knit.
Row 4: K1, p29, k2tog, p29, k1 (61 sts).

PLACING BEADS
Row 1: K1, k2tog tbl, k23, (bead 1, k1)
twice, k2, (bead 1, k1) twice, knit to
last 3 sts, k2tog, k1 (59 sts).
Row 2 & all WS rows: K1, purl to last
st, k1.
Row 3: K24, (bead 1, k1) 6 times, knit
to end.
Row 5: K25, (bead 1, k1) 5 times, knit
to end.
Row 7: K1, k2tog tbl, k21, (bead 1, k1)
6 times, knit to last 3 sts, k2tog, k1
(57 sts).
Row 9: K12, (k2tog tbl, k2) twice, k4,
(bead 1, k1) 5 times, k6, (k2tog, k2)
twice, knit to end (53 sts).
Row 11: K11, (k2 tog tbl, k2) twice, k4,

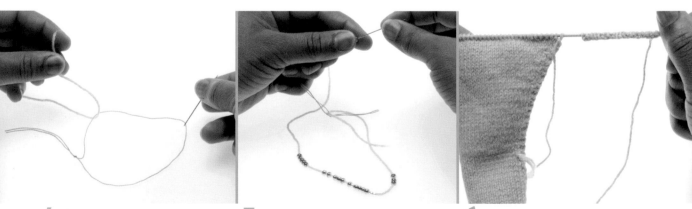

 Thread a sewing needle with
thread and knot the ends to
form a loop. Pass the end of
the yarn through the loop.

5 Thread the beads onto the needle,
then push them down over the
thread and onto the yarn. Make
sure you thread the beads in the
correct color sequence.

6 Using the beaded yarn, cast 19 sts
onto the same needle as the first
side of the slipper.

(bead 1, k1) 4 times, k5, (k2tog, k2) twice, knit to end (49 sts).

Row 13: K10, (k2tog tbl, k2) twice, k4, (bead 1, k1) 3 times, k5, (k2tog, k2) twice, knit to end (45 sts).

Row 15: K9, (k2tog tbl, k2) twice, k5, bead 1, k7, (k2tog, k2) twice, knit to end (41 sts).

Row 17: K8, (k2tog tbl, k2) twice, k4, bead 1, k6, (k2tog, k2) twice, knit to end (37 sts).

Row 19: K7, (k2tog tbl, k2) twice, k9, (k2tog, k2) twice, knit to end (33 sts).

Row 21: K6, (k2tog tbl, k2) twice, k7, (k2tog, k2) twice, knit to end (29 sts).

Row 22: K1, purl to last st, k1.
Bind off knitwise.

FINISHING

Weave in any loose ends to WS on all pieces, then block and steam gently. With RS together, fold the slipper lengthwise so that sides match, then sew the heel and foot seam using a fine backstitch. Turn RS out and fold so that the seam is at the center. Overcast the toe seam on the RS.

 SEE STEPS 8–9

SEE ALSO
Knitting with beads, page 33

7 After finishing the second side, join the two sides together by working straight across all the stitches.

8 With RS together, sew the heel and foot seam using a fine backstitch. Take your time to create a narrow seam so that the slippers are comfortable to wear.

9 Turn the slippers RS out and position the seam so that the love-heart motif is on top, then overcast the toe seam.

Ribbon-and-lace stockings

This project is knitted from the toe up and uses the magic loop technique on a circular needle. Worked in a fine kid mohair/silk blend yarn, the stockings are beautifully soft and gently shaped at center front and back. They are finished with sheer ribbon laced through holes, which fasten on the thigh when worn.

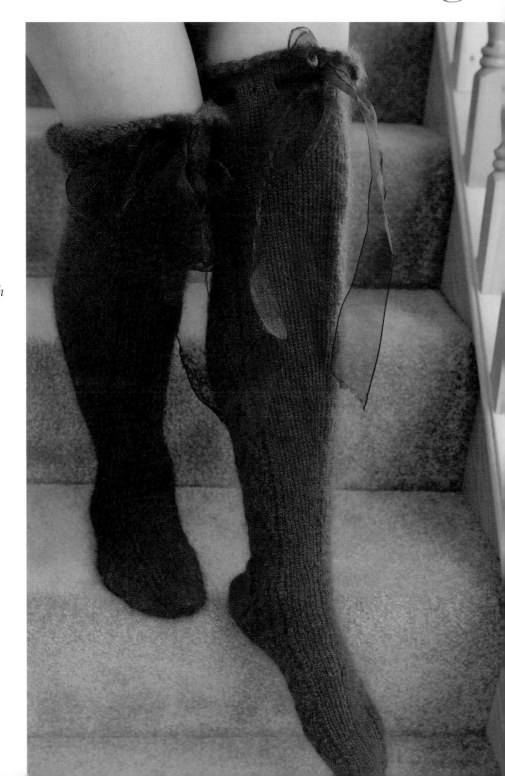

KNITTING THE STOCKINGS (MAKE 2)

Using a size 5 (3.75 mm) circular needle and yarn doubled, cast on 20 sts and follow the pattern using the magic loop technique. In this case, start by pulling the cord between the 11th and 12th stitches. Place a marker in front of the 1st stitch and continue as follows.

Round 1: Knit.

Round 2: (K4, m1k, k2, m1k, k4) twice (24 sts).

Round 3: (K5, m1k, k2, m1k, k5) twice (30 sts).

Round 4: (K6, m1k, k2, m1k, k6) twice (32 sts).

Round 5: (K7, m1k, k2, m1k, k7) twice (36 sts).

Round 6: (K8, m1k, k2, m1k, k8) twice (40 sts).

Round 7: Knit.

Round 8: (K9, m1k, k2, m1k, k9) twice (44 sts).

Round 9: Knit.

Round 10: (K10, m1k, k2, m1k, k10) twice (48 sts).

Rounds 11–14: Knit.

Begin working in lace pattern as follows.

Round 15: [K6, (k2tog, yo) twice, k4, k2tog, yo, k1, yo, k2tog tbl, k5] twice.

Round 16: Knit.

Round 17: [K6, k2tog, yo, k1, (k2tog, yo, k2) twice, yo, k2tog tbl, k5] twice.

Round 18: Knit.

Round 19: [K6, k2tog, yo, k2, (k2tog, yo) twice, k3, yo, k2tog tbl, k5] twice.

Round 20: Knit.

Round 21: [K6, k2tog, yo, k3, k2tog, yo, k4, yo, k2tog tbl, k5] twice.

Round 22: Knit.

 SEE STEPS 1–3

BEFORE YOU START

MEASUREMENTS

Length from heel to toe: 9½ in. (24 cm)

Length from top to heel: 20 in. (50 cm)

YARN

Light-weight yarn (70% super kid mohair, 30% silk; approx. 229 yds/ 210 m per 1 oz/25 g ball) x 5 balls (pink)

Yarn is used doubled throughout

OTHER MATERIALS

Two 1 yd (1 m) lengths of 2-in. (5-cm) wide pink organza ribbon

NEEDLES

32-in. (80-cm) long size 5 (3.75 mm) circular needle

GAUGE

26 sts x 38 rows = 4 in. (10 cm) in stockinette stitch using size 5 (3.75 mm) needle and yarn doubled

ABBREVIATIONS

k—knit; **m1k**—make 1 stitch knitwise; **p**—purl; **RS**—right side; **sl**—slip stitch from left to right needle without working it; **st(s)**—stitch(es); **tbl**—through back of loop; **tog**—together; **WS**—wrong side; **yo**—yarn over

1 Start the lace pattern on row 15. The lace holes are formed using a combination of yarn overs and working two stitches together.

2 When working two stitches together, make sure that you do so through the front or back of the loops (as here) in order to create the correct pattern.

3 As you continue working the lace pattern, notice how the lace holes are positioned. Once you have worked the pattern repeat a couple of times, you will find it easy to spot any mistakes.

Rounds 23–78: Repeat rounds 15–22 seven times.

Rounds 79–82: Repeat rounds 15–18 once.

Round 83: K10, (k2tog, yo) twice, k3, yo, k2tog tbl, k11, k2tog, yo, k2, (k2tog, yo) twice, knit to end.

Round 84: Knit.

HEEL FLAP

Knit the first 9 sts of round, turn work, purl these 9 sts, then purl next 7 sts. These 16 sts form the heel flap. Work backward and forward in rows on these sts only as follows.

Row 1: (K1, sl 1) across heel flap.

Row 2: Purl.

Repeat rows 1–2 until heel is as long as it is wide (about 18 rows).

HEEL TURN

Row 1: (K1, sl 1) 5 times, k1, turn.

Row 2: P6 and turn.

Row 3: (Sl 1, k1) twice, sl 1, k2tog, sl 1, turn.

Row 4: P6, p2tog, p1, turn.

Row 5: (K1, sl 1) 3 times, k1, k2tog, k1, turn.

Row 6: P8, p2tog, p1, turn.

Row 7: (Sl 1, k1) 4 times, sl 1, k2tog, turn.

Row 8: P9, p2tog (10 sts).

GUSSET

Next row: (Sl 1, k1) across 10 sts of heel, pick up and knit 10 sts down left side of heel flap, then place marker in stitch below next stitch on left needle tip.

Continue in pattern to other side of heel as follows: K2, k2tog, yo, k4, yo, k2tog tbl, k11, k2tog, yo, k3, k2tog, yo, k4, place marker in stitch below stitch just worked on right needle, pick up and knit 10 sts up right side of heel, k5 to center of heel (62 sts).

Slide all sts down onto cord, find center 2 sts, and pull cord through to divide sts equally onto both sides of cord. The beginning of the round is at the center back of the heel while you work the gusset. Resume the magic loop technique and work in rounds as follows.

Round 1: Knit to st just before one holding marker, k2tog, knit to next marker, knit st with marker together with next st tbl, knit to end.

Round 2: (K1, sl 1) twice, k8, k2tog, yo, k5, k2tog, yo, k1, yo, k2tog tbl, k11, (k2tog, yo) twice, k6, yo, k2tog tbl, k8, (sl 1, k1) twice, sl 1.

Round 3: As round 1 (58 sts).

Round 4: (K1, sl 1) twice, k7, k2tog, yo, k4, k2tog, yo, k2, yo, k2tog tbl, k11, k2tog, yo, k1, k2tog, yo, k5, yo, k2tog tbl, k7, (sl 1, k1) twice, sl 1.

Round 5: As round 1 (56 sts).

Round 6: (K1, sl 1) twice, k6, (k2tog, yo, k3) twice, yo, k2tog tbl, k11, k2tog, yo, k2, k2tog, yo, k4, yo, k2tog tbl, k6, (sl 1, k1) twice, sl 1.

Round 7: As round 1 (54 sts).

Round 8: (K1, sl 1) twice, k5, k2tog, yo, k2, k2tog, yo, k4, yo, k2tog tbl, k11, (k2tog, yo, k3) twice, yo, k2tog tbl, k5, (sl 1, k1) twice, sl.

Round 9: As round 1 (52 sts).

4 To work the picot bind-off, bind off 3 sts knitwise. *Cast on 3 sts using the cable cast-on method.

5 Bind off the next 6 sts knitwise. Repeat from * until you have bound off all the stitches, then fasten off the yarn.

6 Thread the ribbon through a large yarn needle and use the needle to pass the ribbon in and out through the eyelet holes at the top of the stocking.

SEE ALSO
Circular knitting using magic loop technique, page 31

Round 10: (K1, sl 1) twice, k4, k2tog, yo, k5, k2tog, yo, k1, yo, k2tog tbl, k11, (k2tog, yo) twice, k6, yo, k2tog tbl, k4, (sl 1, k1) twice, sl 1.

Round 11: As round 1 (50 sts).

Round 12: (K1, sl 1) twice, k3, k2tog, yo, k4, k2tog, yo, k2, yo, k2tog tbl, k11, k2tog, yo, k1, k2tog, yo, k5, yo, k2tog tbl, k3, (sl 1, k1) twice, sl 1.

Round 13: As round 1 (48 sts).

LEG

Round 1: K5, k2tog, yo, k4, k2tog, yo, k3, yo, k2tog tbl, k11, k2tog, yo, k2, k2tog, yo, k5, yo, k2tog tbl, k6.

Round 2: Knit.

Round 3: [K5, k2tog, yo, k3, k2tog, yo, k4, yo, k2tog tbl, k6] twice.

Round 4: Knit.

Round 5: [K5, (k2tog, yo) twice, k4, k2tog, yo, k1, yo, k2tog tbl, k6] twice.

Round 6: Knit.

Round 7: [K5, k2tog, yo, k1, (k2tog, yo, k2) twice, yo, k2tog tbl, k6] twice.

Round 8: Knit.

Round 9: [K5, k2tog, yo, k2, (k2tog, yo) twice, k3, yo, k2tog tbl, k6] twice.

Round 10: Knit.

Round 11: [K5, k2tog, yo, k3, k2tog, yo, k4, yo, k2tog tbl, k6] twice.

Round 12: Knit.

Round 13: As round 5.

Round 14: Knit.

Round 15: As round 7.

Round 16: Knit.

Round 17: As round 9.

Round 18: Knit.

Round 19: As round 11.

Start the leg shaping as follows.

Round 20: (K1, place marker on needle, m1k, k22, m1k, place marker on needle, k1) twice (52 sts).

Rounds 21–148: Repeat rounds 5–20 seven times, slipping markers as you come to them and working extra sts in stockinette stitch to keep the lace panels vertical (84 sts).

Rounds 149–164: Work another 16 rounds in pattern but without further shaping (that is, repeat rounds 5–20 but knit round 20 instead of adding sts).

Round 165 (eyelet row): K1, (k2tog, yo, k2) to last 3 sts, k2tog, yo, k1.

Work 1¼ in. (3 cm) in stockinette stitch, then bind off using the picot technique.

 SEE STEPS 4–5

FINISHING

Weave in any loose ends to WS on all pieces; do not block or steam. With WS together, overcast the toe seam. Turn RS out and thread the ribbon through the eyelet holes.

 SEE STEP 6

PROJECT 13

Lace-panel socks

This basic sock shape knitted on two needles is given a feminine look by working lace panels up the leg section and along the upper foot. Lots of different looks can be achieved by lengthening the rib, changing the color, or working more plain rows between the lace rows.

KNITTING THE SOCKS (MAKE 2)

Using size 2 (2.75 mm) needles and yarn A, cast on 57 sts. Break off yarn A and join yarn B.

Row 1 (RS): (P1, k1) to last st, p1.

Row 2: (K1, p1b) to last st, k1.

Rows 3–5: Repeat rows 1–2 once, then row 1 again.

Row 6: (K1, p1b) to last st, k1f&b (58 sts).

 SEE STEPS 1–3

LACE PANELS

Change to size 3 (3.25 mm) needles.

Row 1 (RS): K7, *k2tog, yo, k2, yo, k2tog tbl, k8, k2tog, yo*, k12; repeat from * to * once, then knit to end.

 SEE STEPS 4–6 OVERLEAF

Row 2 & all WS rows: Purl.

Row 3: K6, *k2tog, yo, k4, yo, k2tog tbl, k6, k2tog, yo*, k12; repeat from * to * once, then knit to end.

Row 5: K7, *k2tog, yo, k4, yo, k2tog tbl, k6, k2tog, yo*, k12; repeat from * to * once, then knit to end.

Row 7: K6, *k2tog, yo, k6, yo, k2tog tbl, (k1, k2tog, yo) twice*, k12; repeat from * to * once, then knit to end.

Row 9: K7, *k2tog, yo, k7, k2tog, yo, k3, k2tog, yo*, k12; repeat from * to * once, then knit to end.

Row 11: K6, *k2tog, yo, k7, k2tog, yo, k3, k2tog, yo*, k12; repeat from * to * once, then knit to end.

Row 13: K7, *k2tog, yo, k2, yo, k2tog tbl, k1, k2tog, yo, k5, k2tog, yo*, k12; repeat from * to * once, then knit to end.

Row 15: K6, *k2tog, yo, k4, yo, k2tog tbl, k6, k2tog, yo, k1, k2tog, k7, k2tog tbl, k2tog, yo, k4, yo, k2tog tbl, k6, k2tog, yo, knit to end (56 sts).

Row 17: K7, *k2tog, yo, k4, yo, k2tog tbl, k6, k2tog, yo*, k10; repeat from * to * once, then knit to end.

Row 19: K6, *k2tog, yo, k6, yo, k2tog tbl, (k1, k2tog, yo) twice*, k10; repeat from * to * once, then knit to end.

Row 21: K7, *k2tog, yo, k7, k2tog, yo, k3, k2tog, yo*, k10; repeat from * to * once, then knit to end.

Row 23: K6, *k2tog, yo, k7, k2tog, yo, k3, k2tog, yo*, k10; repeat from * to * once, then knit to end.

Row 25: K7, *k2tog, yo, k2, yo, k2tog tbl, k1, k2tog, yo, k5, k2tog, yo*, k10; repeat from * to * once, then knit to end.

BEFORE YOU START

MEASUREMENTS

Length from heel to toe: 9 in. (23 cm)

Length from top to heel: 7¾ in. (19.5 cm)

YARN

DK-weight yarn (100% merino wool; approx. 175 yds/160 m per 2 oz/50 g ball) in 2 colors:

A Khaki x small amount for casting on

B Green x 1 ball

NEEDLES

Size 2 (2.75 mm)

Size 3 (3.25 mm)

GAUGE

24 sts x 36 rows = 4 in. (10 cm) in stockinette stitch using size 3 (3.25 mm) needles

ABBREVIATIONS

k—knit; **k1f&b**—knit into front and back of same stitch; **p**—purl; **p1b**—purl 1 stitch together with stitch in row below; **RS**—right side; **st(s)**—stitch(es); **tbl**—through back of loop; **tog**—together; **WS**—wrong side; **yo**—yarn over

1 To work p1b in the rib section, insert the right needle purlwise into the stitch one row below the next stitch on the left needle.

2 Complete the purl stitch in the usual way, pulling the yarn through the stitch in the row below and then slipping the next stitch on the current row off the left needle.

3 At the end of the rib section, increase by one stitch using k1f&b. To do this, simply knit into the front and then the back of the next stitch.

Row 27: K6, *k2tog, yo, k4, yo, k2tog tbl, k6, k2tog, yo*, k10; repeat from * to * once, then knit to end.

Row 29: K7, *k2tog, yo, k4, yo, k2tog tbl, k6, k2tog, yo, k2tog, k5, k2tog tbl, k1, k2tog, yo, k4, yo, k2tog tbl, k6, k2tog, yo, knit to end (54 sts).

Row 31: K6, *k2tog, yo, k6, yo, k2tog, (k1, k2tog tbl, yo) twice*, k8; repeat from * to * once, then knit to end.

Row 33: K7, *k2tog, yo, k7, k2tog, yo, k3, k2tog, yo*, k8; repeat from * to * once, then knit to end.

Row 35: K6, *k2tog, yo, k7, k2tog, yo, k3, k2tog, yo*, k8; repeat from * to * once, then knit to end.

Row 37: K7, *k2tog, yo, k2, yo, k2tog tbl, k1, k2tog, yo, k5, k2tog, yo*, k8; repeat from * to * once, then knit to end.

Row 39: K6, *k2tog, yo, k4, yo, k2tog tbl, k6, k2tog, yo*, k8; repeat from * to * once, then knit to end.

Row 41: K7, *k2tog, yo, k4, yo, k2tog tbl, k6, k2tog, yo*, k8; repeat from * to * once, then knit to end.

Row 43: K6, *k2tog, yo, k6, yo, k2tog tbl, (k1, k2tog, yo) twice, k1, k2tog, k3, k2tog tbl, k2tog, yo, k6, yo, k2tog tbl, (k1, k2tog, yo) twice, knit to end (52 sts).

Row 45: K7, *k2tog, yo, k7, k2tog, yo, k3, k2tog, yo*, k6; repeat from * to * once, then knit to end.

Row 47: K6, *k2tog, yo, k7, k2tog, yo, k3, k2tog, yo*, k6; repeat from * to * once, then knit to end.

Row 49: K7, *k2tog, yo, k2, yo, k2tog tbl, k1, k2tog, yo, k5, k2tog, yo*, k6; repeat from * to * once, then knit to end.

Row 51: K6, *k2tog, yo, k4, yo, k2tog tbl, k6, k2tog, yo*, k6; repeat from * to * once, then knit to end.

Row 53: K7, *k2tog, yo, k4, yo, k2tog tbl, k6, k2tog, yo*, k6; repeat from * to * once, then knit to end.

Row 55: K6, *k2tog, yo, k6, yo, k2tog tbl, k4, k2tog, yo*, k6; repeat from * to * once, then knit to end.

Row 56: Purl.

HEEL—FIRST SIDE

Row 1 (RS): K15 and turn.
Row 2 & all WS rows: Purl.
Row 3: K14 and turn.
Row 5: K13 and turn.
Row 7: K12 and turn.
Row 9: K11 and turn.
Row 11: K10 and turn.

Row 13: K9 and turn.
Row 15: K8 and turn.
Row 17: K7 and turn.
Row 19: K8 and turn.
Row 21: K9 and turn.
Row 23: K10 and turn.
Row 25: K11 and turn.
Row 27: K12 and turn.
Row 29: K13 and turn.
Row 31: K14 and turn.
Row 33: K15 and turn.
Row 35: Knit all sts.

👁 **SEE STEPS 7–8**

HEEL—SECOND SIDE
Row 36 (WS): P15 and turn.

👁 **SEE STEP 9**

Row 37 & all RS rows: Knit.
Row 38: P14 and turn.
Row 40: P13 and turn.
Row 42: P12 and turn.
Row 44: P11 and turn.
Row 46: P10 and turn.
Row 48: P9 and turn.
Row 50: P8 and turn.
Row 52: P7 and turn.

4 The lace panels are worked using a combination of stitches, including taking the yarn over (yo) the right needle to create a lace hole. This also creates an extra stitch.

5 Knitting two stitches together (k2tog) decreases one stitch to compensate for the yarn over. It also emphasizes the lace hole, sloping the stitches to the right.

6 Some stitches are knitted together through the back of the loop (k2tog tbl), which slopes the stitches to the left.

Row 54: P8 and turn.

Row 56: P9 and turn.

Row 58: P10 and turn.

Row 60: P11 and turn.

Row 62: P12 and turn.

Row 64: P13 and turn.

Row 66: P14 and turn.

Row 68: Purl all sts.

FOOT

Row 1 (RS): K20, k2tog, yo, k6, k2tog, yo, knit to end.

Row 2: Purl.

Row 3: K21, k2tog, yo, k6, k2tog, yo, knit to end.

Row 4: Purl.

Continue in pattern as set by these 4 rows until foot measures 6 in. (15 cm) from end of heel, ending with row 2 and RS facing for next row.

TOE

Row 1 (RS): K11, k2tog, k2tog tbl, (k6, k2tog, yo) twice, k6, k2tog, k2tog tbl, knit to end (48 sts).

Row 2 & all WS rows: Purl.

Row 3: K10, k2tog, k2tog tbl, k4, (k2tog, yo, k6) twice, k2tog, k2tog tbl, knit to end (44 sts).

Row 5: K9, k2tog, k2tog tbl, k4, k2tog, yo, k6, k2tog, yo, k4, k2tog, k2tog tbl, knit to end (40 sts).

Row 7: K8, k2tog, k2tog tbl, k2, k2tog, yo, k6, k2tog, yo, k4, k2tog, k2tog tbl, knit to end (36 sts).

Row 9: K7, k2tog, k2tog tbl, k2, k2tog, yo, k6, k2tog, yo, k2, k2tog, k2tog tbl, knit to end (32 sts).

Row 11: K6, k2tog, k2tog tbl, k2tog, yo, k6, k2tog, yo, k2, k2tog, k2tog tbl, knit to end (28 sts).

Row 13: K5, k2tog, k2tog tbl, k10, k2tog, k2tog tbl, knit to end (24 sts).

Row 15: K4, k2tog, k2tog tbl, k8, k2tog, k2tog tbl, knit to end (20 sts).

Row 17: K3, k2tog, k2tog tbl, k6, k2tog, k2tog tbl, knit to end (16 sts).

Bind off purlwise.

FINISHING

Weave in any loose ends to WS on all pieces, then block and steam gently except for the rib. Fold the sock lengthwise RS together and sew the back seam using a fine backstitch. Turn RS out and fold so that the seam is at center back of the sock. Overcast the toe seam on the RS.

7 Start the first side of the heel by knitting 15 sts. Turn the work at the end of these stitches and continue the heel using short-row shaping as instructed in the pattern.

8 Short-row shaping will produce this rounded heel piece. When completed, knit across all the stitches in the row to reach the other side of the sock.

9 Start the second side of the heel by purling 15 sts. Turn the work at the end of these stitches and continue the heel using short-row shaping in the same way as for the first side.

 **PROJECT 14**

Top-seam socks

These socks, worked in alpaca yarn on two needles, are a variation on project 13, but have the seam on top of the sock instead of at the back. The seam is turned into a decorative feature by working lace holes down the side edges. The decorative detailing and softness of the yarn mean that these socks are best worn for relaxing.

1 The lace pattern on these socks is very simple. Start each RS row by knitting the first stitch, then knitting two stitches together (k2tog).

KNITTING THE SOCKS (MAKE 2)

Using size 3 (3.25 mm) needles, cast on 58 sts.

Row 1 (RS): (P1, k1 tbl) to end.

Row 2: (P1 tbl, k1) to end.

Rows 3–8: Repeat rows 1–2 three times. Change to size 5 (3.75 mm) needles and begin placing the lace holes.

Row 9 (RS): K1, (k2tog, yo) twice, knit to last 6 sts, (k2tog, yo) twice, k2.

Row 10: Purl.

Rows 11–66: Repeat rows 9–10 fifty-eight times.

 **SEE STEPS 1–2**

HEEL

Row 1 (RS): K1, (k2tog, yo) twice, k36, wrap st, turn.

 **SEE STEPS 3–4**

Row 2: P23, wrap st, turn.

SEE STEPS 5–6 OVERLEAF

Row 3: K22, wrap st, turn.

Row 4: P21, wrap st, turn.

Row 5: K20, wrap st, turn.

Row 6: P19, wrap st, turn.

Row 7: K18, wrap st, turn.

Row 8: P17, wrap st, turn.

Row 9: K16, wrap st, turn.

Row 10: P15, wrap st, turn.

Row 11: K14, wrap st, turn.

Row 12: P13, wrap st, turn.

On following rows, work each wrap bar and slip stitch together as one.

Row 13: K14 and turn.

SEE STEPS 7–8 OVERLEAF

Row 14: P15 and turn.

Row 15: K16 and turn.

Row 16: P17 and turn.

Row 17: K18 and turn.

Row 18: P19 and turn.

Row 19: K20 and turn.

Row 20: P21 and turn.

Row 21: K22 and turn.

Row 22: P23 and turn.

Row 23: Knit to last 6 sts, (k2tog, yo) twice, k2.

Row 24. Purl all sts.

FOOT

Beginning with a knit row, continue working in stockinette stitch with lace holes at the side edges as set by previous rows until foot measures

BEFORE YOU START

MEASUREMENTS

Length from heel to toe: 9¼ in. (23.5 cm)

Length from top to heel: 8¾ in. (22 cm)

YARN

DK-weight yarn (100% alpaca; approx. 131 yds/120 m per 2 oz/50 g ball) x 2 balls (lilac)

NEEDLES

Size 3 (3.25 mm)

Size 5 (3.75 mm)

GAUGE

24 sts x 32 rows = 4 in. (10 cm) in stockinette stitch using size 5 (3.75 mm) needles

ABBREVIATIONS

k—knit; **p**—purl; **RS**—right side; **st(s)**—stitch(es); **tbl**—through back of loop; **tog**—together; **wrap st**—see steps 3–8; **WS**—wrong side; **yo**—yarn over

2 Bring the yarn to the front of the work, then take it over the needle (yo) to work the next k2tog. Work another yo, then knit to the other side of the sock for the second half of the lace pattern.

3 To work a wrap stitch on a RS row, bring the yarn to the front of the work and slip the next stitch from the left to the right needle without working it.

4 Take the yarn to back of work, then pass the slip stitch from the right needle back onto the left one. You have now completed a wrap stitch.

6¼ in. (16 cm) from end of heel, ending with WS facing for next row.

Next row (WS): P5, p2tog, purl to last 7 sts, p2tog, purl to end (56 sts).

TOE

Row 1 (RS): K1, (k2tog, yo) twice, k6, k2tog, k2, k2tog tbl, k22, k2tog, k2, k2tog tbl, knit to last 6 sts, (k2tog, yo) twice, k2 (52 sts).

Row 2: Purl.

Row 3: K1, (k2tog, yo) twice, k5, k2tog, k2, k2tog tbl, k20, k2tog, k2, k2tog tbl, knit to last 6 sts, (k2tog, yo) twice, k2 (48 sts).

Row 4: Purl.

Row 5: K1, (k2tog, yo) twice, k4, k2tog, k2, k2tog tbl, k18, k2tog, k2, k2tog tbl, knit to last 6 sts, (k2tog, yo) twice, k2 (44 sts).

Row 6: Purl.

Row 7: K1, (k2tog, yo) twice, k3, k2tog, k2, k2tog tbl, k16, k2tog, k2, k2tog tbl, knit to last 6 sts, (k2tog, yo) twice, k2 (40 sts).

Row 8: Purl.

Row 9: K1, (k2tog, yo) twice, k2, k2tog, k2, k2tog tbl, k14, k2tog, k2, k2tog tbl, knit to last 6 sts, (k2tog, yo) twice, k2 (36 sts).

Row 10: P6, p2tog tbl, p2, p2tog, p12, p2tog tbl, p2, p2tog, purl to end (32 sts).

Row 11: K1, k2tog, yo, k2, k2tog, k2, k2tog tbl, k10, k2tog, k2, k2tog tbl, k1, k2tog, yo, k2 (28 sts).

Row 12: P4, p2tog tbl, p2, p2tog, p8, p2tog tbl, p2, p2tog, purl to end. Bind off knitwise.

FINISHING

Weave in any loose ends to WS on all pieces, then block and steam gently except for the rib. Fold the sock lengthwise RS together and sew the top seam using a fine backstitch. Turn RS out and fold so that seam is at center front. Overcast the toe seam on the RS.

 SEE STEPS 9–10

5 To work a wrap stitch on a WS row, take the yarn to the back of the work and slip the next stitch from the left to the right needle without working it.

6 Bring the yarn to front of the work, then pass the slip stitch from the right needle back onto the left one. You have now completed a wrap stitch.

7 Work each wrap bar and slip stitch together as one to avoid gaping at the turn of the heel. Use the tip of the right needle to lift the wrap bar and transfer it onto the left needle.

8 Insert the right needle into both the wrap bar and slip stitch on the left needle and work together, knitwise on a RS row (as here) and purlwise on a WS row.

9 Fold the sock RS together and sew the top seam using a fine backstitch.

10 Turn RS out, fold the sock so that seam is at center top, then overcast the toe seam on the RS.

PROJECT 15

Stripy lace socks

These socks combine richly colored stripes with lace and are knitted in a luxuriously soft wool/cashmere blend yarn on double-pointed needles. The rib, heel, and toes are plain, making it easier to shape these sections and providing a contrast to the stripes.

KNITTING THE SOCKS (MAKE 2)

Using size 3 (3.25mm) needles and yarn B, cast on 60 sts and divide evenly onto three dpns. Place a marker at the first stitch to mark the beginning of the round.

 **SEE STEPS 1–2**

Break off yarn B and join yarn A. Work in k1, p1 rib for ¾ in. (2 cm). Break off yarn A and continue on size 5 (3.75 mm) needles.
Rounds 1–2: Using yarn B, knit to end. Without breaking off yarn B, join yarn C.

1 Cast 60 sts onto a double-pointed needle, then transfer the first 20 sts onto a second dpn. Without twisting the needles, transfer the next 20 sts onto a third dpn.

Round 3: Using yarn C, (k2tog, yo) to end.

Round 4: Knit to end.

Without breaking off yarn C, join yarn D.

Rounds 5–6: Using yarn D, knit to end.

Rounds 7–30: Repeat rounds 1–6 four times.

👁 **SEE STEPS 3–4**

Round 31: Using yarn B, k1, k2tog, knit to last 3 sts, k2tog, k1 (58 sts).

Round 32: Knit to end.

Rounds 33–36: Repeat rounds 3–6 once.

Rounds 37–48: Repeat rounds 31–36 twice (54 sts).

Rounds 49–52: Repeat rounds 31–34 once (52 sts).

HEEL FLAP

Break off yarns B and C.

Using yarn D, k9, then slide these sts along to other end of this dpn and transfer them onto the previous dpn. This needle should now hold 25 sts, comprising 9 sts in yarn D and 16 sts in yarn C.

With a spare dpn, take 7 sts in yarn C from the end of this needle, leaving 18 sts for the heel, with marker at the center. Rearrange the remaining 34 sts evenly onto two dpns. These will form the instep and will be worked later.

👁 **SEE STEPS 5–6 OVERLEAF**

BEFORE YOU START

MEASUREMENTS

Length from heel to toe: 9 in. (23 cm)

Length from top to heel: 9 in. (23 cm)

YARN

DK-weight yarn (57% merino wool, 33% microfiber, 10% cashmere; approx. 142 yds/130 m per 2 oz/50 g ball) in 4 colors:

A Pale pink x 1 ball

B Hot pink x 1 ball

C Orange x 1 ball

D Red x 1 ball

NEEDLES

Four size 5 (3.75 mm) double-pointed needles

Four size 3 (3.25 mm) double-pointed needles

GAUGE

28 sts x 30 rows = 4 in. (10 cm) in stockinette stitch using size 5 (3.75 mm) needles

ABBREVIATIONS

dpn(s)—double pointed needle(s); **k**—knit; **p**—purl; **RS**—right side; **st(s)**—stitch(es); **tbl**—through back of loop; **tog**—together; **WS**—wrong side; **yo**—yarn over

2 Arrange the needles in a triangle, with the stitches evenly divided. Place a marker made from scrap yarn at the first stitch to indicate the beginning of the round.

3 The lace pattern is very simple. Start by knitting two stitches together (k2tog) in the usual way.

4 Bring the yarn to the front of the work and then wrap it over the right needle (yo). Continue alternating k2tog and yo all around the sock.

Place a marker in front of the first stitch on the heel needle; this marks the new start of rounds.

Round 1: Knit.

Continue working on the 18 heel sts only. Working back and forth in rows, and beginning and ending with a purl row, work in stockinette stitch until heel is 2 in. (5 cm) long.

 SEE STEP 7

HEEL TURN

Row 1 (RS): K12 and turn.

Row 2: P6 and turn.

Row 3: K5, k2tog, k1, turn.

Row 4: P6, p2tog, p1, turn.

Row 5: K7, k2tog, k1, turn.

Row 6: P8, p2tog, p1, turn.

Row 7: K9, k2tog, k1, turn.

Row 8: P10, p2tog, p1, turn (12 sts).

 SEE STEP 8

GUSSET

1st dpn: K12 across heel sts, then pick up and knit 13 sts down the side of the heel and place a marker.

2nd dpn: K22 from instep.

3rd dpn: K12 from instep, place a marker, then pick up and knit 13 sts up the other side of the heel (72 sts).

 SEE STEPS 9–10

Round 1: Knit to within 3 sts of next marker, k2tog, k1, slip marker, knit to next marker, k1, k2tog tbl, knit to end (70 sts). Without breaking off yarn D, join yarn B.

Rounds 2–3: Using yarn B, repeat round 1 twice (66 sts). Without breaking off yarn B, join yarn C.

Round 4: Using yarn C, (k2tog, yo) to within 3 sts of next marker, k1, k2tog, slip marker, k1, (yo, k2tog) to next marker, k2tog, k1, slip marker, knit to end (64 sts).

Round 5: Still using yarn C, repeat round 1 (62 sts).

Round 6: Using yarn D, repeat round 1 (60 sts).

Rounds 7–10: Repeat rounds 1–4 once (52 sts).

Round 11: Using yarn C, knit to end.

Round 12: Using yarn D, knit to end.

Rounds 13–54: Continue in stripe sequence, without decreasing.

Round 55: Using yarn D, knit to end.

Break off all yarns.

TOE

Slip the first 6 sts of round onto the previous dpn. Join yarn A.

Round 1: Using yarn A and the 1st dpn—k13; 2nd dpn—k26; 3rd dpn—k13. Place a marker to indicate the beginning of the round at the center sole position.

Round 2: K10, k2tog, k2, k2tog, k20, k2tog, k2, k2tog, k10 (48 sts).

Round 3: Knit.

Round 4: K9, k2tog, k2, k2tog, k18, k2tog, k2, k2tog, k9 (44 sts).

5 Rearrange the stitches in order to work the heel. When transferring stitches from one needle to another, take care not to twist them.

6 Arrange the stitches so there are 34 sts in yarn C evenly divided onto two dpns (these will form the instep). The third dpn should have 9 sts each in yarns C and D for the heel.

7 Working on the 18 heel stitches only, work the first part of the heel in rows of stockinette stitch until it is 2 in. (5 cm) long.

SEE ALSO
Circular knitting using dpns, page 30

Round 5: Knit.

Round 6: K8, k2tog, k2, k2tog, k16, k2tog, k2, k2tog, k8 (40 sts).

Round 7: Knit.

Round 8: K7, k2tog, k2, k2tog, k14, k2tog, k2, k2tog, k7 (36 sts).

Round 9: K6, k2tog, k2, k2tog, k12, k2tog, k2, k2tog, k6 (32 sts).

Round 10: K5, k2tog, k2, k2tog, k10, k2tog, k2, k2tog, k5 (28 sts).

Round 11: K4, k2tog, k2, k2tog, k8, k2tog, k2, k2tog, k4 (24 sts).

Round 12: K6, then slip these sts onto previous dpn.

Hold the 12 sts on both dpns RS together and use a spare dpn to bind off both sets of sts together purlwise.

FINISHING

Weave in any loose ends to WS on all pieces, then steam gently.

8 Work in short rows to shape the bottom of the heel turn.

9 To start working in rounds again to work the foot of the sock, use a spare dpn to pick up and knit 13 sts down the first side of the heel.

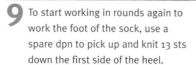

10 Place a marker, knit the stitches of the instep, place another marker, then pick up and knit 13 sts up the other side of the heel.

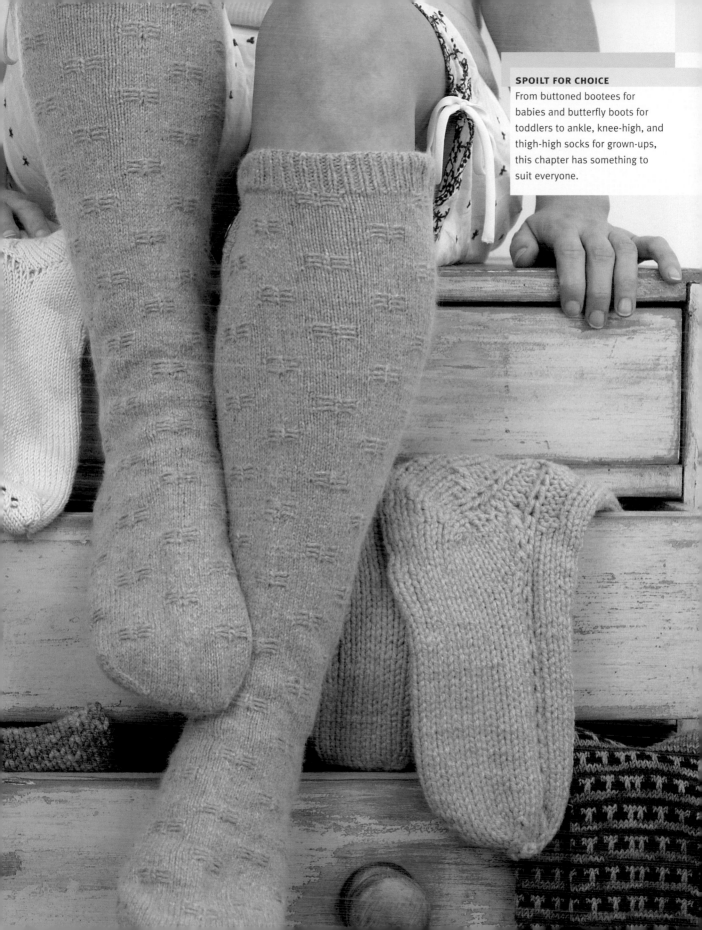

SPOILT FOR CHOICE
From buttoned bootees for
babies and butterfly boots for
toddlers to ankle, knee-high, and
thigh-high socks for grown-ups,
this chapter has something to
suit everyone.

PROJECT 16

Knee-high socks

These knee-high socks are worked from the top down in a cashmere/ cotton blend yarn that gives them both softness and strength. The soft yarn is subtly enhanced with a pretty butterfly texture pattern.

SHAPING THE LEG

There is no shaping on the leg section of these socks so that they will stretch more tightly around the calf to help them stay up. However, if you have large calves or would simply prefer to shape the legs, knit the first third of the leg on needles two sizes larger than that specified in the pattern—that is, size 4 (3.5 mm)—then change to needles one size larger—that is, size 3 (3 mm)—for the next third. Complete the final third of the leg using the correct needle size—that is, size 2 (2.5 mm). Measure your leg circumference below the knee, at the calf, and at the ankle. Knit some test gauge swatches with the different needle sizes, and adjust as necessary to obtain a good fit, remembering that the socks need to stretch around the legs to stay up.

KNITTING THE SOCKS (MAKE 2)

Using size 2 (2.5 mm) dpns, cast on 70 sts and divide as evenly as possible onto three dpns; or using a size 2 (2.5 mm) circular needle, cast on 70 sts and divide evenly into two sets of stitches.

 SEE STEPS 1–2

Round 1: (K1, p1) to end.
Repeat round 1 until top rib measures 1¼ in. (3 cm), increasing by k1f&b at end of last round (71 sts).

LEG

Begin working in butterfly texture as follows.
Round 1: K2, *(yf, sl 3, yb, k1) twice, k12, repeat from * to last 9 sts, (yf, sl 3, yb, k1) twice, k1.
Round 2: Knit.
Rounds 3–6: Repeat rounds 1–2 twice.
Rounds 7–10: Knit.

 SEE STEPS 3–4 OVERLEAF

Round 11: *K12, (yf, sl 3, yb, k1) twice, repeat from * to last 11 sts, knit to end.
Round 12: Knit.
Rounds 13–16: Repeat rounds 11–12 twice.
Rounds 17–20: Knit.
Rounds 21–140: Work in pattern as set by rounds 1–20 until another six repeats have been completed.
Rounds 141–150: Repeat rounds 1–10 once.

HEEL FLAP

Knit the next 9 sts of round, then turn. Purl back across the next 18 sts, then turn.
If you are working on a circular needle, you will probably need to move sts along the needle and pull cord through between different sts in order to continue working in rows.
Beginning with a knit row, work backward and forward in stockinette stitch until heel flap is as long as it is wide (about 32 rows), ending with RS facing.

BEFORE YOU START

MEASUREMENTS
Length from heel to toe: 9 in. (23 cm)
Length from top to heel: 14 in. (35.5 cm)

YARN
Sport-weight yarn (35% cotton, 25% polyamide, 18% angora, 13% viscose, 9% cashmere; approx. 197 yds/180 m per 2 oz/50 g ball) x 4 balls (lilac)
Small amount of yarn in a contrasting color for grafting the toes

NEEDLES
Four size 2 (2.5 mm) double-pointed needles **OR**
One 32-in. (80-cm) long size 2 (2.5 mm) circular needle

GAUGE
31 sts x 50 rows = 4 in. (10 cm) in butterfly texture pattern using size 2 (2.5 mm) needles

ABBREVIATIONS
dpn(s)—double-pointed needle(s); **k**—knit; **k1f&b**—knit into front and back of same stitch; **p**—purl; **RS**—right side; **sl**—slip stitch from left needle to right needle without working it; **st(s)**—stitch(es); **tbl**—through back of loop; **tog**—together; **yb**—take yarn between needles to back of work; **yf**—bring yarn between needles to front of work; **WS**—wrong side

PATTERN NOTE
This pattern includes instructions for making the socks using either double-pointed needles or the magic loop technique with a circular needle. Choose whichever method you prefer.

1 **Using dpns:** Cast on 70 sts and divide them as evenly as possible onto three dpns—that is, 23 sts each on two dpns and 24 sts on the third dpn.

2 **Using circular needle:** Cast on 70 sts and pull the cord through between the center two stiches. Slide one half of the stitches onto the left needle tip and leave the other half on the cord.

HEEL TURN

Row 1: K12, turn.

Row 2: P7, turn.

Row 3: K6, k2tog, k1, turn.

Row 4: P7, p2tog, p1, turn.

Row 5: K8, k2tog, k1, turn.

Row 6: P9, p2tog, p1, turn.

Row 7: K10, k2tog, k1, turn.

Row 8: P11, p2tog, turn (12 sts).

GUSSET

Knit 12 sts across heel flap, pick up and knit 10 sts down left side of heel (work into the back of the sts to eliminate any holes that may occur), place marker, k3, *(yf, sl 3, yb, k1) twice, k12, repeat from * once, then (yf, sl 3, yb, k1) twice, k2, place marker, pick up and knit 10 sts up right side of heel flap (work into back of sts as before). Knit to center of heel (85 sts).

If using dpns, arrange sts over 3 dpns as evenly as possible. If using a circular needle, slide all the sts down onto cord, find center 2 sts, and pull cord through between them to divide sts into 2 sets. With both techniques, the beginning of the round will now be at the center of the heel.

 **SEE STEPS 5–6**

Round 1: Knit to within 2 sts of marker, k2tog, slip marker, knit to next marker, slip marker, k2tog tbl, knit to end (83 sts).

Round 2: Knit to marker, slip marker, k3, *(yf, sl 3, yb, k1) twice, k12, repeat from * once, then (yf, sl 3, yb, k1) twice, k3, slip marker, knit to end.

Round 3: As round 1 (81 sts).

Rounds 4–5: Repeat rounds 2–3 once (79 sts).

Round 6: Knit all sts, slipping markers as you come to them.

Round 7: As round 1 (77 sts).

Round 8: As round 6.

Round 9: As round 1 (75 sts).

Round 10: Knit to marker, slip marker, k13, *(yf, sl 3, yb, k1) twice, k12, repeat from * once, slip marker, knit to end.

Round 11: As round 1 (73 sts).

Round 12: As round 10.

Round 13: As round 1 (71 sts).

Round 14: As round 10.

Round 15: As round 1 (69 sts).

Round 16: As round 6.

Round 17: As round 1 (67 sts).

Round 18: As round 6.

Round 19: As round 1 (65 sts).

FOOT

Continue working without decreasing any more sts. With beginning of round at center base of foot, place butterfly texture as follows.

Round 1: K9, *(yf, sl 3, yb, k1) twice, k12, repeat from * once then (yf, sl 3, yb, k1) twice, knit to end.

Round 2: Knit.

Rounds 3–6: Repeat rounds 1–2 twice.

Rounds 7–10: Knit.

Round 11: K19, [(yf, sl 3, yb, k1) twice, k12] twice, knit to end.

Round 12: Knit.

Rounds 13–16: Repeat rounds 11–12 twice.

Rounds 17–20: Knit.

Continue in pattern as set by rounds 1–20 until foot measures 6¼ in. (16 cm) from end of heel, decreasing one stitch in last round (64 sts).

TOE

If using dpns, knit the first 16 sts of next round. If using a circular needle, knit the first 16 sts of next round, then slide all sts down onto cord and divide so there are 32 sts on each side. Pull cord between center 2 sts. For both dpns and circular needle, the beginning of the round should now be at the side of the toe.

 SEE STEPS 7–8

3 **Using dpns or circular needle:** Work the butterfly texture by bringing the yarn to the front, slipping 3 sts, and then taking the yarn to the back again.

4 **Using dpns or circular needle:** Alternate the row of butterfly texture with rows of knit to build up the pattern.

5 **Using dpns:** Rearrange the stitches on the needles to start working the gusset and foot. The start of the round should now be at the center of the heel.

SEE ALSO
Circular knitting, pages 30–31
Grafting, page 24

Continue working in rounds, shaping the toe as follows.

Round 1: (K2tog tbl, k28, k2tog) twice (60 sts).

Round 2: Knit.

Round 3: (K2tog tbl, k26, k2tog) twice (56 sts).

Round 4: Knit.

Round 5: (K2tog tbl, k24, k2tog) twice (52 sts).

Round 6: Knit.

Round 7: (K2tog tbl, k22, k2tog) twice (48 sts).

Round 8: Knit.

Round 9: (K2tog tbl, k20, k2tog) twice (44 sts).

Round 10: (K2tog tbl, k18, k2tog) twice (40 sts).

Round 11: (K2tog tbl, k16, k2tog) twice (36 sts).

Round 12: (K2tog tbl, k14, k2tog) twice (32 sts).

Round 13: (K2tog tbl, k12, k2tog) twice (28 sts).

Round 14: (K2tog tbl, k10, k2tog) twice (24 sts).

Break off yarn and join in contrast colored yarn. Knit in rounds of this yarn for about 1¼ in. (3 cm). This forms a "chimney" to make grafting the toe easier.

FINISHING

Weave in any loose ends to WS on all pieces, then block and steam gently. Graft the toes, then remove the chimney.

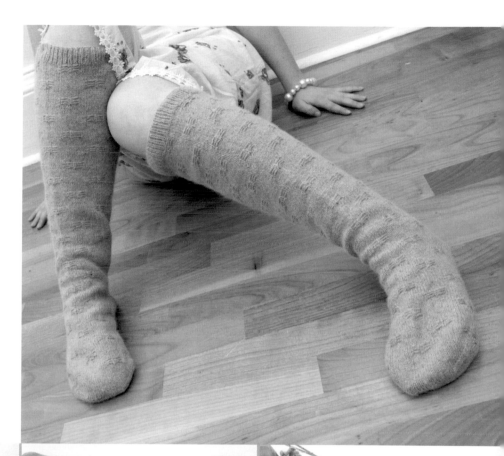

6 **Using circular needle:** Divide the stitches evenly onto the two needles, with start of round at center of heel. Pull the right needle through to work the next round.

7 **Using dpns:** Knit the first 16 sts of the next round to get the stitches onto the correct dpns for shaping the toe. The start of the round is now at the side of the toe.

8 **Using circular needle:** Knit the first 16 sts of next round, then divide the stitches so there are 32 sts in each half. Pull the cord through, ready to shape the toe.

PROJECT 17

Beaded legwarmers

These legwarmers are knitted in the round on sets of four double-pointed needles using a bulky-weight wool blend yarn, with beaded accents on the ribbing. The legwarmers will slide easily over shoes, making sure you stay warm in the coldest of winters, but you could knit them in cotton for warmer weather.

KNITTING THE LEGWARMERS (MAKE 2)

Thread 64 beads onto the yarn.

 SEE STEP 1

Using size 9 (5.5 mm) double-pointed needles, cast on 40 sts. Divide the sts onto three needles as follows:

1st dpn: 14 sts.
2nd dpn: 12 sts.
3rd dpn: 14 sts.

Place a marker after last st on 3rd dpn. Work in rounds throughout.

Rounds 1–2: P1, (k3, p2) to within 4 sts of marker, k3, p1.
Round 3: P1, *k1, bead 1, k1, p2; repeat from * to within 4 sts of marker, k1, bead 1, k1, p1.

 SEE STEPS 2–3

Round 4: P1, (k3, p2) to within 4 sts of marker, k3, p1.
Rounds 5–11: Repeat rounds 3–4 three times, then round 3 once.
Round 12: P1, m1k, (k3, p2) 7 times, k3, m1k, p1 (42 sts).

Change to size 10 (6 mm) needles and knit every row until work measures 12 in. (30 cm) from end of rib.
Next round: K1, k2tog, k36, k2tog, k1 (40 sts).
Change to size 9 (5.5 mm) needles and repeat rounds 3–4 three times. Bind off knitwise, taking care not to do so too tightly.

FINISHING

Weave in any loose ends to WS on all pieces, then block and steam gently except for the beaded ribbing.

BEFORE YOU START

MEASUREMENTS

15 in. (33 cm) long x 12½ in. (32 cm) circumference

YARN

Bulky-weight yarn (50% merino wool, 50% acrylic; approx. 60 yds/55 m per 2 oz/50 g ball) x 5 balls (variegated pink/orange)

BEADS

128 x 5 mm clear glass beads

NEEDLES

Four size 9 (5.5 mm) double-pointed needles
Four size 10 (6 mm) double-pointed needles

GAUGE

13 sts x 19 rows = 4 in. (10 cm) in stockinette stitch using size 10 (6 mm) double-pointed needles

ABBREVIATIONS

bead 1—place 1 bead; **k**—knit; **m1k**—make 1 stitch knitwise; **p**—purl, **st(s)**—stitch(es); **tog**—together **WS**—wrong side

1 Thread a sewing needle with thread, tie a knot to form a loop, then slip the end of yarn through the loop. Slide the beads down the needle and onto the yarn.

2 Work the instruction bead 1 by bringing the yarn to the front, sliding a bead up the yarn, then slipping the next stitch purlwise from left to right needle.

3 Take the yarn to the back again so that the bead sits in front of the slip stitch. Continue placing beads in this way in the ribbing.

PROJECT 18

Mock-cable socks

Worked from the top down, these chunky socks are knitted in a strong wool/synthetic blend yarn, making them quick to knit and durable to wear. This is a great project for learning how to shape socks using the magic loop technique. The cable effect on the side of the sock is created by combining knit and purl stitches with a tied technique rather than true cabling.

KNITTING THE SOCKS (MAKE 2)

Using a size 10 (6 mm) circular needle, cast on 36 sts and follow the pattern using the magic loop technique.

Rounds 1–6: K1, p1 to end.

Begin working mock-cable pattern.

Round 7: [K3, p3, (sl 1k, p3) twice, k4] twice.

Round 8: [K3, p3, (k1, p3) twice, k4] twice.

Rounds 9–12: Repeat rounds 7–8 twice.

Round 13: [K3, p3, tie st, p3, k4] twice.

 SEE STEPS 1–3

Round 14: [K3, p3, (k1, p3) twice, k4] twice.

Round 15: [K3, p3, (sl 1k, p3) twice, k4] twice.

Round 16: [K3, p3, (k1, p3) twice, k4] twice.

Rounds 17–24: Repeat rounds 15–16 four times.

Rounds 25–36: Repeat rounds 13–24 once.

Rounds 37–46: Repeat rounds 13–22 once.

HEEL FLAP

Work the next 9 sts as follows.

Row 1: K3, p3, sl 1k, p2, turn.

You will probably need to move sts along needle and pull cord through between different sts in order to continue working in rows on the circular needle.

Row 2: K2, p1, k3, p3, p2tog, p2, k3, p1, m1k, k1.

These 18 sts form the heel flap.

(eye icon) **SEE STEP 4 OVERLEAF**

Continue working backward and forward in rows on these 18 sts only as follows.

Row 3: P2, sl 1k, p3, k6, p3, sl 1k, p2.

Row 4: K2, p1, k3, p6, k3, p1, k2.

Row 5: P2, sl 1k, p2, k8, p2, sl 1k, p2.

Row 6: K2, p1, k2, p8, k2, p1, k2.

Row 7: P2, sl 1k, p1, k10, p1, sl 1k, p2.

Row 8: K2, p1, k1, p10, k1, p1, k2.

Row 9: P2, sl 1k, k12, sl 1k, p2.

Row 10: K2, p14, k2.

Row 11: P1, k16, p1.

Row 12: P18.

BEFORE YOU START

MEASUREMENTS

Length from heel to toe: 10 in. (25 cm)
Length from top to heel: 9½ in. (24 cm)

YARN

Bulky weight yarn (50% merino, 50% acrylic; approx. 60 yds/55 m per 2 oz/50 g ball) x 4 balls (green)

NEEDLES

1-yd (1-m) long size 10 (6 mm) circular needle
Bulky cable needle

GAUGE

13 sts x 19 rows = 4 in. (10 cm) in stockinette stitch using size 10 (6 mm) needle

ABBREVIATIONS

k—knit; **m1k**—make 1 stitch knitwise; **p**—purl; **RS**—right side; **sl 1k**—slip 1 stitch knitwise from left to right needle without working it; **st(s)**—stitch(es); **tbl**—through back of loop; **tie st**—see steps 1–3; **tog**—together; **WS**—wrong side

1 Work tie stitch by slipping 5 sts onto the cable needle and holding them at the back of the work.

2 Wrap the yarn counterclockwise twice around the 5 sts on the cable needle.

3 Return the 5 sts to the left needle, then work them as follows: sl 1k, p3, sl 1k.

HEEL TURN

Row 1: K12, turn.

Row 2: P6, turn.

Row 3: K5, k2tog, k1, turn.

Row 4: P6, p2tog, p1, turn.

Row 5: K7, k2tog, k1, turn.

Row 6: P8, p2tog, p1, turn.

Row 7: K9, k2tog, k1, turn.

Row 8: P10, p2tog, p1, turn (12 sts).

 SEE STEP 5

GUSSET

Knit 12 sts across heel flap, then pick up and knit 9 sts down left side of heel, working into the back of each stitch to eliminate any holes that may occur. Place a marker.

Sliding stitches onto cord as necessary to make knitting easier, work the next 18 sts as follows:

P1, sl 1k, p2, k9, p2, sl 1k, p2tog, place marker, pick up and knit 9 sts up right side of heel, working into the back of stitches as before (47 sts).

Knit 6 sts to center of heel.

 SEE STEP 6

Slide all sts onto cord, find center 2 sts, and pull the cord through to divide the sts equally onto each half of cord. The beginning of the round is now at the center back of the heel when working the gusset.

 SEE STEP 7

Resuming the magic loop technique, work in rounds as follows.

Round 1: Knit to within 2 sts of marker, k2tog, slip marker, p1, k1, p1, k11, p1, k1, p1, slip marker, k2tog tbl, knit to end.

Round 2: Knit to marker, slip marker, p1, sl 1k, p1, k11, p1, sl 1k, p1, slip marker, knit to end.

Round 3: Knit to within 2 sts of marker, k2tog, slip marker, p1, k1, p1, k11, p1, k1, p1, slip marker, k2tog tbl, knit to end.

Round 4: Knit to marker, slip marker, p1, sl 1k, p1, k11, p1, sl 1k, p1, slip marker, knit to end.

Round 5: Knit to within 2 sts of marker, k2tog, slip marker, p1, k1, p1, k11, p1, k1, p1, slip marker, k2tog tbl, knit to end.

Round 6: Knit to marker, slip marker, p1, sl 1k, p1, k11, p1, sl 1k, p1, slip marker, knit to end.

Rounds 7–10: Repeat rounds 5–6 twice (37 sts).

FOOT

The beginning of the round is now at the base of the foot.

 SEE STEP 8

Continue in pattern without decreasing as follows.

Round 1: K10, p1, k1, p1, k11, p1, k1, p1, k10.

Round 2: K10, p1, sl 1k, p1, k11, p1, sl 1k, p1, k10.

Repeat rounds 1–2 until foot measures 7 in. (18 cm) long from end of heel shaping. Finish with a repeat of round 1.

TOE

Knit the first 9 sts of round. Slide all sts onto cord and divide so that there are 19 sts on left and 18 sts on right side of cord. Pull cord through between both sets of sts. The beginning of the round is now at the side of the toe.

4 Move the stitches along the cord and needle as necessary until you have the 18 heel sts in place for working the heel flap.

5 Work in short rows to shape and turn the heel flap. When you have completed the short-row shaping, you should have 12 sts on the needle, ready to work the gusset.

6 Join the heel flap to the rest of the stitches for working the gusset by picking up and knitting 12 sts along each side of the flap, placing markers where indicated.

SEE ALSO
Circular knitting using magic loop technique, page 31
Grafting, page 24

Round 1: K8, k2tog tbl, knit to end of round (36 sts).

Round 2: (K1, k2tog tbl, k12, k2tog, k1) twice (32 sts).

Round 3: Knit.

Round 4: (K1, k2tog tbl, k10, k2tog, k1) twice (28 sts).

Round 5: (K1, k2tog tbl, k8, k2tog, k1) twice (24 sts).

Round 6: (K1, k2tog tbl, k6, k2tog, k1) twice (20 sts).

Round 7: (K1, k2tog tbl, k4, k2tog, k1) twice (16 sts).

Do not bind off. Graft the toe seam.

 SEE STEP 9

FINISHING

Weave in any loose ends to WS on all pieces, then block and steam gently.

7 Divide the stitches evenly on the circular needle so that the start of the round is at the center of the heel for working the gusset.

8 When you start to work the foot, the beginning of the round should be at the base of the foot.

9 Do not bind off when you have finished knitting the sock. Instead, divide the remaining stitches onto both needle tips and use a yarn needle to graft the seam.

PROJECT 19

Stripy Fair Isle socks

These socks are much easier than working real Fair Isle. They are based on the basic two-needle sock shape (such as projects 13 and 14), but are worked in a four-color stripe sequence with slipped stitches to give a Fair Isle look. This technique produces a denser fabric than you would normally get from stockinette stitch, which guarantees that the socks are warm and cozy to wear.

KNITTING THE SOCKS (MAKE 2)

Using size 2 (2.75 mm) needles and yarn D, cast on 71 sts. Without breaking off yarn D, join yarn A.

Row 1 (RS): Using yarn A, (k1, p1) to last st, k1.

Row 2: (P1, k1) to last st, p1. Join yarn B.

Row 3: Using yarn B, (k1, p1) to last st, k1.

Row 4: (P1, k1) to last st, p1. Join yarn C.

Row 5: Using yarn C, (k1, p1) to last st, k1.

Row 6: (P1, k1) to last st, p1. Join yarn D.

Row 7: Using yarn D, (k1, p1) to last st, k1.

Row 8: (P1, k1) to last st, p1.

Rows 9–16: Repeat rows 1–8 once, carrying yarns up side of work and taking care not to pull them too tightly.

 SEE STEP 1

LEG

Keeping the sequence of colors as set by rib, begin working the 2-row slip-stitch stripes.

Row 1 (RS): K1, m1k, knit to last st, m1k, k1 (73 sts).

Row 2 & all unspecified WS rows: Purl.

Row 3: Knit.

Row 5: K4, (sl 1, k3) to last st, k1.

Row 6: P4, (sl 1, p3) to last st, p1.

Row 7: K2, (sl 1, k3) to last 3 sts, sl 1, k2.

Row 8: P2, (sl 1, p3) to last 3 sts, sl 1, p2.

 **SEE STEPS 2–3**

Row 9: K23, k2tog, k23, k2tog tbl, knit to end (71 sts).

Row 11: Knit.

Row 13: K4, [(sl 1, k3) 5 times, k3] twice, (sl 1, k3) to last st, k1.

Row 14: P4, [(sl 1, p3) 5 times, p3] twice, (sl 1, p3) to last st, p1.

Row 15: K2, *(sl 1, k3) 5 times, sl 1, k2; repeat from * to end.

Row 16: P2, *(sl 1, p3) 5 times, sl 1, p2; repeat from * to end.

SEE STEPS 4–5 OVERLEAF

Rows 17 & 19: Knit.

Row 21: K4, (sl 1, k3) 4 times, sl 1, k1, k2tog, k3, (sl 1, k3) 5 times, k2tog tbl, k1, (sl 1, k3) to last st, k1 (69 sts).

Row 22: P4, [(sl 1, p3) 4 times, sl 1, p5] twice, (sl 1, p3) 5 times, p1.

Row 23: K2, [(sl 1, k3) 5 times, sl 1, k1] twice, (sl 1, k3) to last 3 sts, sl 1, k2.

Row 24: P2, [(sl 1, p3) 5 times, sl 1, p1] twice, (sl 1, p3) to last 3 sts, sl 1, p2.

Rows 25 & 27: Knit.

Row 29: K4, [(sl 1, k3) 5 times, k2] twice, (sl 1, k3) to last st, k1.

Row 30: P4, [(sl 1, p3) 5 times, p2] twice, (sl 1, p3) to last st, p1.

Row 31: As row 23.

Row 32: As row 24.

Row 33: K21, k2tog, k23, k2tog tbl, knit to end (67 sts).

Row 35: Knit.

Row 37: K4, [(sl 1, k3) 5 times, k1] twice, (sl 1, k3) to last st, k1.

Row 38: P4, [(sl 1, p3) 5 times, p1] twice, (sl 1, p3) to last st, p1.

Row 39: K2, (sl 1, k3) 5 times, k1, (sl 1, k3) 6 times, k1, (sl 1, k3) to last 3 sts, sl 1, k2.

Row 40: P2, (sl 1, p3) 5 times, p1, (sl 1, p3) 6 times, p1, (sl 1, p3) to last 3 sts, sl 1, p2.

Rows 41 & 43: Knit.

Row 45: K4, (sl 1, k3) 4 times, k2tog, (k3, sl 1) 5 times, k3, k2tog tbl, (k3, sl 1) to last 4 sts, k4 (65 sts).

BEFORE YOU START

MEASUREMENTS

Length from heel to toe: 11 in. (28 cm)

Length from top to heel: 10¼ in. (26 cm)

YARN

DK-weight yarn (100% merino wool; approx. 175 yds/160 m per 2 oz/50 g ball) in 4 colors:

A Brown marl x 2 balls

B Charcoal x 2 balls

C Mustard x 2 balls

D Burgundy x 2 balls

NEEDLES

Size 2 (2.75 mm)

GAUGE

31 sts x 45 rows = 4 in. (10 cm) in pattern using size 2 (2.75 mm) needles

ABBREVIATIONS

k—knit; **m1k**—make 1 stitch knitwise; **p**—purl; **RS**—right side; **st(s)**—stitch(es); **sl**—slip stitch from left to right needle without working it; **tbl**—through back of loop; **tog**—together; **wrap st**—see pages 97–99 (steps 3–8); **WS**—wrong side

1 Carry the yarns not in use up the side of the work instead of breaking them off and rejoining them later. This will save you from having to weave in lots of ends.

2 Work the slip-stitch pattern that creates the Fair Isle look by combining knit and slip stitches on RS rows.

3 Use a combination of purl and slip stitches on WS rows, keeping the yarn on the WS of the work whenever you slip a stitch.

Row 46: P4, (sl 1, p3) 4 times, p4, (sl 1, p3) 5 times, p4, (sl 1, p3) to last st, p1.

Row 47: K2, (sl 1, k3) to last 3 sts, sl 1, k2.

Row 48: P2, (sl 1, p3) to last 3 sts, sl 1, p2.

Rows 49 & 51: Knit.

Row 53: K4, (sl 1, k3) to last st, k1.

Row 54: P4, (sl 1, p3) to last st, p1.

Row 55: As row 47.

Row 56: As row 48.

Row 57: K19, k2tog, k23, k2tog tbl, knit to end (63 sts).

Row 59: Knit.

Row 61: K4, (sl 1, k3) 4 times, k3, (sl 1, k3) 5 times, k3, (sl 1, k3) to last st, k1.

Row 62: P4, (sl 1, p3) 4 times, p3, (sl 1, p3) 5 times, p3, (sl 1, p3) to last st, p1.

Row 63: K2, (sl 1, k3) 4 times, sl 1, k2, (sl 1, k3) 5 times, sl 1, k2, (sl 1, k3) to last 3 sts, sl 1, k2.

Row 64: P2, (sl 1, p3) 4 times, sl 1, p2, (sl 1, p3) 5 times, sl 1, p2, (sl 1, p3) to last 3 sts, sl 1, p2.

Rows 65 & 67: Knit.

Row 69: K4, (sl 1, k3) 3 times, sl 1, k1, k2tog, (k3, sl 1) 5 times, k3, k2tog tbl, k1, (sl 1, k3) to last st, k1 (61 sts).

Row 70: P4, (sl 1, p3) 4 times, p2, (sl 1, p3) 5 times, p2, (sl 1, p3) 4 times, p1.

Row 71: K2, (sl 1, k3) 4 times, sl 1, k1, (sl 1, k3) 5 times, sl 1, k1, (sl 1, k3) to last 3 sts, sl 1, k2.

Row 72: P2, (sl 1, p3) 4 times, sl 1, p1, (sl 1, p3) 5 times, sl 1, p1, (sl 1, p3) to last 3 sts, sl 1, p2.

Rows 73 & 75: Knit.

Row 77: K4, (sl 1, k3) 4 times, k2, (sl 1, k3) 5 times, k2, (sl 1, k3) to last st, k1.

Row 78: P4, (sl 1, p3) 4 times, p2, (sl 1, p3) 5 times, p2, (sl 1, p3) to last st, p1.

Row 79: As row 71.

Row 80: P2tog, (sl 1, p3) 4 times, sl 1, p1, (sl 1, p3) 5 times, sl 1, p1, (sl 1, p3) to last 3 sts, sl 1, p2 (60 sts).

Break off all yarns except yarn A, then work the heel using yarn A only.

HEEL—FIRST SIDE

Row 1 (RS): K15, wrap st, turn.

Row 2 & all WS rows: Purl.

Row 3: K14, wrap st, turn.

Row 5: K13, wrap st, turn.

Row 7: K12, wrap st, turn.

Row 9: K11, wrap st, turn.

Row 11: K10, wrap st, turn.

Row 13: K9, wrap st, turn.

Row 15: K8, wrap st, turn.

On following rows, work each wrap bar and slip stitch together as one.

Row 17: K9 and turn.

Row 19: K10 and turn.

Row 21: K11 and turn.

Row 23: K12 and turn.

4 Continue the slip-stitch pattern up the leg section. Here, row 15 is being worked using yarn D, while stitches of yarn C from the previous row are slipped.

5 On the following WS row, the stitches that were slipped on row 15 are slipped once again. Take care to slip the correct stitches so that the Fair Isle pattern emerges correctly.

SEE ALSO
Wrap stitch, pages 97–99
(steps 3–8)

Row 25: K13 and turn.
Row 27: K14 and turn.
Row 29: K15 and turn.
Row 31: Knit all sts.

HEEL—SECOND SIDE

Row 1 (WS): P15, wrap st, turn.
Row 2 & all RS rows: Knit.
Row 3: P14, wrap st, turn.
Row 5: P13, wrap st, turn.
Row 7: P12, wrap st, turn.
Row 9: P11, wrap st, turn.
Row 11: P10 wrap st, turn.
Row 13: P9, wrap st, turn.
Row 15: P8, wrap st, turn.
On following rows, work each wrap bar and slip stitch together as one.
Row 17: P9 and turn.
Row 19: P10 and turn.
Row 21: P11 and turn.
Row 23: P12 and turn.
Row 25: P13 and turn.
Row 27: P14 and turn.
Row 29: P15 and turn.
Row 31: Purl all sts.
Without breaking off yarn A, rejoin yarn B.

FOOT

Row 1 (RS): Using yarn B, knit.
Row 2: Purl. Rejoin yarn C.
Row 3: Using yarn C, k4, (sl 1, k3) 4 times,

k2, (sl 1, k3) 5 times, k2, (sl 1, k3) 4 times.
Row 4: P3, (sl 1, p3) 4 times, p2, (sl 1, p3) 5 times, p2, (sl 1, p3) 4 times, p1.
Rejoin yarn D.
Row 5: Using yarn D, k2, (sl 1, k3) 4 times, sl 1, k1, (sl 1, k3) 5 times, sl 1, k1, (sl 1, k3) 4 times, sl 1, k1.
Row 6: P1, (sl 1, p3) 4 times, sl 1, p1, (sl 1, p3) 5 times, sl 1, p1, (sl 1, p3) 4 times, sl 1, p2.
Row 7: Using yarn A, knit.
Row 8: Purl.
Continue in pattern as set by these 8 rows until foot measures 7 in. (18 cm) from end of heel, ending after a repeat of row 8. Break off all colors except yarn A.

TOE

Row 1 (RS): K12, k2tog, k2, k2tog tbl, k24, k2tog, k2, k2tog tbl, knit to end (56 sts).

 SEE STEP 6

Row 2 & all unspecified WS rows: Purl.
Row 3: Knit.
Row 5: K11, k2tog, k2, k2tog tbl, k22, k2tog, k2, k2tog tbl, knit to end (52 sts).
Row 7: Knit.
Row 9: K10, k2tog, k2, k2tog tbl, k20, k2tog, k2, k2tog tbl, knit to end (48 sts).
Row 11: K9, k2tog, k2, k2tog tbl, k18, k2tog, k2, k2tog tbl, knit to end (44 sts).

Row 13: K8, k2tog, k2, k2tog tbl, k16, k2tog, k2, k2tog tbl, knit to end (40 sts).
Row 14: P7, p2tog tbl, p2, p2tog, p14, p2tog tbl, p2, p2tog, purl to end (36 sts).
Row 15: K6, k2tog, k2, k2tog tbl, k12, k2tog, k2, k2tog tbl, knit to end (32 sts).
Row 16: P5, p2tog tbl, p2, p2tog, p10, p2tog tbl, p2, p2tog, purl to end (28 sts).
Bind off remaining sts knitwise.

 SEE STEP 7

FINISHING

Weave in any loose ends to WS on all pieces, then block and steam gently. Fold the sock lengthwise RS together and sew the back seam using a fine backstitch. Turn RS out and fold so that the seam is at center back. Overcast the toe seam on the RS.

 SEE STEP 8

6 Decrease the number of stitches at the start of the toe section by working two stitches together using k2tog or k2tog tbl and yarn A.

7 When you have finished working the toe, bind off the remaining stitches knitwise.

8 After you have sewn the back seam using a fine backstitch, turn the sock RS out and overcast the toe seam. Keep the seam fine for a comfortable fit.

PROJECT 20

Slip-stitch rib socks

Worked in an alpaca/wool blend yarn, these thick, comfy socks are perfect for keeping your feet warm, whether you are out hiking or relaxing at home on a chilly day. The slip-stitch rib pattern gives the socks a rich texture that enhances their cozy appeal.

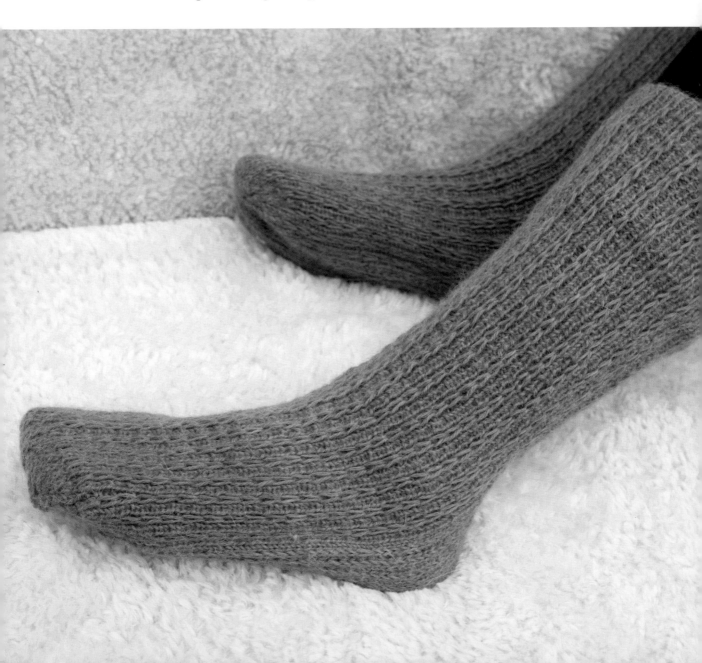

KNITTING THE SOCKS (MAKE 2)

Using size 3 (3 mm) needles, cast on 84 sts and divide as evenly as possible onto three dpns. Place a marker onto the needle to mark the beginning of the round.

 SEE STEP 1

Rounds 1–6: (P1, k1) to end.
Begin working in slip-stitch rib as follows.
Rounds 7–9: (P1, sl 1, p1, k1) to end.
Round 10: (P1, k1) to end.
Continue in slip-stitch rib as set by rounds 7–10 until sock measures 7 in. (18 cm) from end of k1, p1 rib (about 84 rounds), ending with round 10.

 SEE STEPS 2–3

HEEL FLAP

Work 27 sts of next round to create the heel flap as follows.
Row 1 (RS): (Sl 1, k1) 13 times, sl 1, turn.
Row 2: P27, turn.

 SEE STEP 4 OVERLEAF

Working backward and forward in rows on these 27 sts only, continue in slip-stitch pattern as set by rows 1–2 until the heel is as long as it is wide (about 26 rows).

HEEL TURN

Row 1 (RS): (Sl 1, k1) 9 times, sl 1, turn.
Row 2: P11, turn.
Row 3: (Sl 1, k1) 5 times, k2tog, k1, turn.
Row 4: P11, p2tog, p1 turn.
Row 5: (K1, sl 1) 6 times, k2tog, k1, turn.
Row 6: P13, p2tog, p1, turn.
Row 7: (Sl 1, k1) 7 times, k2tog, k1, turn.
Row 8: P15, p2tog, p1, turn.
Row 9: (Sl 1, k1) 8 times, k2tog, k1, turn.
Row 10: P17, p2tog, p1 (19 sts).

GUSSET AND FOOT

Work across the 19 sts of heel flap as follows: (sl 1, k1) 9 times, sl 1. Pick up and knit 12 sts down the left side of the heel, working into the back of each stitch to eliminate any holes that may occur. Place marker, k1, *p1, sl 1, p1, k1; repeat from * until there is 1 stitch before the other side of the heel flap, then k1 and place marker.

BEFORE YOU START

MEASUREMENTS
Length from heel to toe: 11 in. (28 cm)
Length from top to heel: 10 in. (25 cm)

YARN
DK-weight yarn (70% alpaca, 30% wool; approx. 289 yds/265 m per 4 oz/100 g ball) x 2 balls (green)

NEEDLES
Four size 3 (3 mm) double-pointed needles

GAUGE
36 sts x 47 rows = 4 in. (10 cm) in patterned rib using of size 3 (3 mm) needles

ABBREVIATIONS
dpn(s)—double-pointed needle(s); **k**—knit; **p**—purl; **RS**—right side; **sl**—slip stitch from left to right needle without working it, with yarn at WS of work; **st(s)**—stitch(es); **tbl**—through back of loop; **tog**—together; **WS**—wrong side

1 Divide the cast-on stitches evenly onto three dpns and place a marker at the beginning of the round.

2 The slip-stitch rib pattern is based on k1, p1 rib, but slips a stitch instead of knitting it at regular intervals. Keep the yarn at the WS of the work when slipping a stitch.

3 Continue the slip-stitch rib pattern, making sure that you work the stitches correctly to build up a regular pattern.

Using a spare dpn, pick up and knit 12 sts up the second side of the heel. Rearrange the stitches as evenly as possible over three dpns so that beginning of round is just right of center heel (100 sts).

 SEE STEPS 5–8

Round 1: Knit to within 2 sts of marker, k2tog, slip marker, work in slip-stitch rib pattern to marker, slip marker, k2tog tbl, knit to end (98 sts).

Round 2: Work in (k1, sl 1) heel pattern to marker, slip marker, work in slip-stitch rib pattern to next marker, slip marker; beginning with sl 1, work in heel pattern to end of round.

Rounds 3–24: Repeat rounds 1–2 eleven times (76 sts).

Continue working in heel pattern and slip-stitch rib pattern as set until foot is 9½ in. (24 cm) long from end of heel. K19, place marker, then knit until there are 19 sts remaining of round. The start of round should now be at the side of the foot for shaping the toe; move the round marker. Rearrange the sts on three dpns as necessary.

 SEE STEP 9

TOE

Round 1: K2tog tbl, (sl 1, k1) to within 2 sts of marker, k2tog, k2tog tbl, (sl 1, k1) to last 2 sts of round, k2tog (72 sts).

Round 2: Knit

Round 3: K2 tog tbl, (k1, sl 1) to within 2 sts of marker, k2tog, k2tog tbl, (k1 , sl 1) to last 2 sts of round, k2tog (68 sts).

Round 4: Knit.

Rounds 5–8: Repeat rounds 1–4 (60 sts).

Round 9: As round 1 (56 sts).

Round 10: Knit.

Round 11: As round 3 (52 sts).

Round 12: K2tog tbl, knit to within 2 sts of marker, k2tog, k2tog tbl, knit to last 2 sts of round, k2tog (48 sts).

Rounds 13–16: Repeat rounds 11–12 twice (32 sts).

Round 17: As round 3 (28 sts).

Rearrange the remaining sts onto two dpns, with start of round at side of foot. Graft the toe seam.

FINISHING

Weave in any loose ends to WS on all pieces, then block and steam gently.

4 Starting the heel by working back and forth in rows across 27 sts.

5 When the heel flap is as long as it is wide, prepare the stitches for working the gusset and foot. Start by working across the heel stitches once more.

6 Pick up and knit 12 sts down the left side of the heel flap. Work into the back of each stitch that you pick up; this will help to prevent any holes from appearing.

SEE ALSO
Circular knitting using dpns,
page 30
Grafting, page 24

7 Place a marker, then work across the instep stitches and place another marker before picking up and knitting stitches up the right side of the heel flap.

8 Make sure that the stitches are arranged as evenly as possible onto three dpns and that the beginning of the next round is just right of the center heel.

9 Before you can shape the toe, you will need to rearrange the stitches on three dpns so that the beginning of the round is at the side of the foot. Move the round marker there.

GIFTS GALORE
Hand-knitted socks make the perfect gift for friends and family. They look good, feel fabulous to wear, and everyone will appreciate the time and care it took to make them.

Yarn directory

Below is a list of the specific yarns used to make the projects. If you cannot find any of these yarns or simply wish to make a project in a different yarn, use the information supplied here to help you choose a suitable alternative. Refer also to the beginning of each project, where you will find the quantity, weight, and fiber content of the yarns used to make them.

NEEDLE SIZE AND GAUGE

The needle size and gauge supplied here are those recommended on the ball band of the yarn. Note that they are NOT the needle size and gauge that you should use to make the projects. Sometimes a project pattern specifies a different needle size and gauge from those recommended by the manufacturer in order to achieve a certain look. The information supplied here is simply to help you select a substitute yarn, if you wish to do so, that matches the weight of the original yarn as closely as possible so that you can achieve comparable results in the finished project.

PROJECT 1: *Textured baby bootees*
Yarn: Lana Grossa Cool Wool 2000; colors & codes: A = Lime Green 481, B = Apricot 478; needles: size 2–4 (3–3.5 mm); gauge: 24 sts x 34 rows.

PROJECT 2: *Stripy toddler toasties*
Yarn: Lana Grossa Cool Wool 2000; colors & codes: A = Green 509, B = Vivid Blue 510; needles: size 2–4 (3–3.5 mm); gauge: 24 sts x 34 rows.

PROJECT 3: *Buttoned baby bootees*
Yarn: RYC Cashcotton 4 Ply; colors & codes: A = Sugar 901 (pink) or Pretty 902 (blue), B = Cream 900; needles: size 3 (3.25 mm); gauge: 28 sts x 36 rows.

PROJECT 4: *Butterfly and bumble boots*
Yarn: Rowan Scottish Tweed DK; colors & codes: butterfly boots A = Brilliant Pink 10, B = Lavender 05, C = Thatch 18; bumble boots A = Midnight 23, B = Thatch 18, C = Porridge 24; needles: size 6 (4 mm); gauge: 20–22 sts x 28–30 rows.

PROJECT 5: *Felted Sunday boots*
Yarns A–D: Rowan Scottish Tweed DK; colors & codes: A = Peat 19, B = Apple 15, C = Lobster 17, D = Thatch 18; needles: size 6 (4 mm); gauge: 20–22 sts x 28–30 rows. Yarn E: Rowan Scottish Tweed 4 Ply; color & code: Rust 09; needles: size 2–3 (3–3.25 mm); gauge: 26–28 sts x 38–40 rows.

PROJECT 6: *Side-seam socks*
Yarn A: Lana Grossa Cool Wool 2000 Print; color & code: Blue 809; needles: size 2–4 (3–3.5 mm); gauge: 24 sts x 34 rows. Yarn B: Lana Grossa Cool Wool Big; color & code: Blue 629; needles: sizes 4–6 (3.5–4 mm); gauge: 19 sts x 26 rows.

PROJECT 7: *Beaded Argyle socks*
Yarn: Rowan 4ply Soft; colors & codes: A = Irish Cream 386, B = Whisper 370, C = Nippy 376; needles: size 3 (3.25 mm); gauge: 28 sts x 36 rows.

PROJECT 8: *Basic tubular socks*
Yarn: Lana Grossa Meilenweit Cotton; color & code: Maya 7018; needles: size 1–2 (2.5–3 mm); gauge: 26 sts x 36 rows.

PROJECT 9: *Spiral heelless socks*
Yarn: Artesano Alpaca Inca Cloud DK; color & code: Lilac 002; needles: size 6 (4 mm); gauge: 25 sts x 33 rows.

PROJECT 10: *Pompom bobby socks*
Yarn A: Regia Stretch 4ply; color & code: Fantasy 82; needles: size 0–3 (2–3 mm); gauge: 30 sts x 42 rows. Yarn B: Jaeger Baby Merino 4ply; color & code: Snowdrop 102; needles: size 3 (3.25 mm); gauge: 28 sts x 36 rows.

PROJECT 11: *Love-heart slippers*
Yarn: RYC Cashcotton 4 Ply; color & code: Sugar 901; needles: size 3 (3.25 mm); gauge: 28 sts x 36 rows.

PROJECT 12: *Ribbon-and-lace stockings*
Yarn: Rowan Kidsilk Haze; color & codes: Blushes 583; needles: size 3–8 (3.25–5 mm); gauge: 18–25 sts x 23–34 rows.

PROJECT 13: *Lace-panel socks*
Yarn: Lana Grossa Cool Wool 2000; colors & codes: A = Khaki 460, B = Pale Green 495; needles: size 2–4 (3–3.5 mm); gauge: 24 sts x 34 rows.

Suppliers

PROJECT 14: *Top-seam socks*
Yarn: Artesano Alpaca Inca Cloud DK; color & code: Lilac 002; needles: size 6 (4 mm); gauge: 25 sts x 33 rows.

PROJECT 15: *Stripy lace socks*
Yarn: RYC Cashsoft DK; colors & codes: A = Bloom 506; B = Madam 511; C = Clementine 510; D = Poppy 512; needles: size 6 (4 mm); gauge: 22 sts x 30 rows.

PROJECT 16: *Knee-high socks*
Yarn: RYC Cashcotton 4 Ply; colors & codes: Chintz 906; needles: size 3 (3.25 mm); gauge: 28 sts x 36 rows.

PROJECT 17: *Beaded legwarmers*
Yarn: Lana Grossa Due Print; color & code: B = Pink/Orange/Gray 502; needles: size 10–10½ (6–7 mm); gauge: 12 sts x 17 rows.

PROJECT 18: *Mock-cable socks*
Yarn: Lana Grossa Mille; color & code: Teal 417; needles: size 10–10½ (6–7 mm); gauge: 12 sts x 15 rows.

PROJECT 19: *Stripy Fair Isle socks*
Yarn A: Lana Grossa Cool Wool 2000 Print; color & code: Brown Marl 718; needles: size 2–4 (3–3.5 mm); gauge: 24 sts x 34 rows. Yarns B–D: Lana Grossa Cool Wool 2000; colors & codes: B = Charcoal 444, C = Camel 476, D = Claret 438; needles: size 2–4 (3–3.5 mm); gauge: 24 sts x 34 rows.

PROJECT 20: *Slip-stitch rib socks*
Yarn: UK Alpaca; color: Moss; needles: size 3–7 (3–4.5 mm); gauge: 21–28 sts x 27–36 rows.

ROWAN AND RYC YARNS
www.knitrowan.com
www.ryclassic.com

Rowan USA
4 Townsend West, Suite 8
Nashua, NH 03064
United States
(603) 886 5041/5043
wfibers@aol.com

Diamond Yarn
155 Martin Ross, Unit 3
Toronto
Ontario M3J 2L9
Canada
(416) 736 6111
diamond@diamondyarn.com

Rowan Yarns UK
Green Lane Mill
Holmfirth
West Yorkshire HD9 2DX
United Kingdom
(01484) 681 881

Australian Country Spinners
314 Albert Street
Brunswick, Victoria 3056
Australia
(03) 9380 3888

Alterknitives
PO Box 47961
New Zealand
(64) 9376 0337

REGIA SOCK YARNS
Coats Crafts UK
PO Box 22, Lingfield House
Lingfield Point
McMullen Road
Darlington DL1 1YQ
United Kingdom
(01325) 394 237
consumer.ccuk@coats.com
www.coatscraft.co.uk

LANA GROSSA YARNS
www.lanagrossa.com

Unicorn Books & Crafts Inc.
1338 Ross Street
Petaluma, CA 94954
United States
(707) 762 3362
help@unicornbooks.com

Estelle Designs
2220 Midland Avenue, Unit 65
Scarborough, Ontario M1P 3E6
Canada
(416) 298 9922
info@estelledesigns.ca

Lana Grossa UK
2 Riverside, Milngavie
Glasgow G62 6PL
Scotland
(0141) 956 3121
sales@lanagrossa.co.uk

Lana Grossa Europe (Headquarters)
Ingolstädter Straße 86
85080 Gaimersheim
Germany
(0) 84 58 61 0
office@lanagrossa.de

ALPACA YARNS
Artesano Ltd
28 Mansfield Rd
Reading, Berkshire RG1 6AJ
United Kingdom
(0118) 950 3350
www.artesano.co.uk

UK Alpaca
Vulscombe Farm
Vulscombe Lane
Cruwys Morchard
Tiverton, Devon EX16 8NB
United Kingdom
(01884) 243 579/(01598) 753 644
enquiries@ukalpaca.com
www.ukalpaca.com

Index

Author's acknowledgments
Thanks to the following people for their help in supplying such beautiful yarns to work with: Fiona Thompson and Marlene Tulloch at Lana Grossa UK; Ann Hinchcliffe and all at Rowan/ Jaeger/RYC in Holmfirth; Tom Coomber at Artesano Ltd; Juliet at UK Alpaca in Devon. To Kate Kirby, Michelle Pickering, Moira Clinch, and all at Quarto, thanks for putting up with all the delays... To my brilliant knitters and friends Anthea McAlpin, Kathleen Dyne, and Carolyn Rattray, I really couldn't have done it without your help and never-ending patience. To James, Cathryn, Jess, Annabel, and the other models, thank you for making socks fun and funky. Finally Julie Marchington, it got done, what do you think? Very finally to my new husband Sam Sloan, thanks as always for your support, patience, and brilliant photography throughout.

All photographs and illustrations are the copyright of Quarto Publishing plc.